The Lawyer's

Quick

Guide To

E-mail

by Kenneth E. Johnson

Law Practice Management Section
American Bar Association

Cover design by Sam Girton.

Contents

To Claire, again and always.

Acknowledgments

My gratitude goes out to the people who made this book possible:

Beverly Loder and Tim Johnson at the ABA helped shepherd this book from proposal to final form, helping immensely in organizing the material into a coherent whole. Their presence in these acknowledgments also means that they didn't make me do too many drafts.

A very big thanks to G. Burgess Allison, the dean of Law Practice Management Section computer writers, for pushing me back on track when the manuscript strayed, and for pointing out where additional information was needed. His books provided much of that additional information. Greg Siskind gave valuable feedback on each draft. His comments were particularly welcome, since Greg has built a very successful practice by effectively using e-mail. I heartily recommend his ABA book *The Lawyer's Guide to Marketing on the Internet* for all lawyers who want to know how to expand their practice through the Internet. And last, but certainly not least, my thanks to Jeff Flax, who provided valuable feedback on the second draft. Jeff, I appreciated the phone calls to clarify things.

Jeff Beard of MicroLaw, Inc., whose detailed technical explanations of the Network2d mailing list make subscribing worthwhile, first pointed out the security issues of checking your e-mail from a Web browser, and he was also one of the first people I know who dug into PGP for Personal Privacy for Eudora. Jeff was my PGP buddy, and we exchanged several encrypted messages as I was learning PGP. Thanks a lot, Jeff, and sorry about the '97 Packers.

And of course, the largest debt of gratitude goes to my daughter, Claire, who accepts "Daddy needs to work on his book" without complaint.

About the Author

Kenneth E. Johnson is Information Services Project Leader at the law firm of Mayer, Brown & Platt in Chicago. His responsibilities include the evaluation of new technologies and their implementation, with a particular emphasis on the firm's Internet/intranet/extranet strategies. He has been with the firm since 1991, serving for five and a half years as Training and Support Manager.

Mr. Johnson is the author of *The Lawyer's Guide to Creating Web Pages,* published by the ABA Law Practice Management Section in 1997. He is assistant editor of *Network 2d,* the newsletter of the Section's Computer and Technology Division Interest Groups, and co-editor of the Section's online newsletter page (http://www.abanet.org/lpm/newsletters/home.html).

Mr. Johnson is a frequent speaker on legal technology and writes regularly about computers and technology for several business and legal computing publications. He is a contributing editor of *Practical Windows* and *DOS World Magazine* and a frequent contributor to *Law Office Computing, WordPerfect for the Law Office, The Internet Lawyer,* and the *Computers for Lawyers* newsletter. He is also a coauthor of *WordPerfect Law Office Solutions for DOS,* 1st and 2nd editions, and *WordPerfect Law Office Solutions for Windows,* 2nd edition, from James Publishing. His articles have appeared in such publications as *Law Practice Management, Legal Assistant Today,* the *LAW MUG* newsletter, *The Small Business Journal, The Computer Journal, Creativity Connection,* and *The WordPerfectionist.* He recently began an online "Retro Technology" column for the On Computers radio show (http://msncomputing.msn.com/OnComputers/Default.ASP). Since 1991 he has written a monthly "Beginner's Column" for the Chicago Computer Society and the Tulsa Computer Society. These columns are made available to other computer users groups worldwide and have been reprinted more than five hundred times. In 1996 he was awarded Best Columnist (Large Newsletters) in the Lotus Newsletter Contest, at the 9th Intergalactic User Group Officers Conference in New York.

Since 1996 Mr. Johnson has been a faculty member at the annual Writer's Institutes at the University of Wisconsin-Madison, presenting on Internet topics. He maintains the WWWScribe Web site (http://www. wwwscribe.com), which is dedicated to helping writers explore new writing and business opportunities by effectively using the Internet and the World Wide Web.

Mr. Johnson holds a master's degree in anthropology and a master's in business administration from the University of Illinois.

Foreword

In 1995, the ABA Section of Law Practice Management launched its popular series of Internet guides with Burgess Allison's runaway best-seller, *The
Lawyer's Guide to the Internet*. This series includes *The Lawyer's Guide to
Marketing on the Internet* by Gregory Siskind and Timothy Moses, *The Lawyer's Guide to Creating Web Pages* by Ken Johnson, *The Lawyer's Quick Guide
to Microsoft Internet Explorer* and *The Lawyer's Quick Guide to Netscape Navigator* by Burgess Allison, *The Internet Fact Finder for Lawyers* by Joshua D.
Blackman with David Jank, and *Law Law Law on the Internet* by Erik Heels
and Richard Klau. These practical tools for lawyers who want to incorpo-
rate this exciting technology into their practices have integrated law offices into McLuhan's global village.

You have probably found that your clients are clamoring for you to
communicate with them through Internet e-mail messaging. You should
also realize that your local counsel, overseas associates, and opposing
counsel are increasingly using e-mail. You may have heard that e-mail
messaging is not a secure form of communication and so have been reluc-
tant to use it for that reason. To address the legal applications of e-mail,
Ken Johnson has produced another book that takes the mystery out of Internet technology and puts it to work for you—in your office, at home, or
on the road.

Mr. Johnson, the Information Services Project Leader for the Chicago
law firm of Mayer, Brown & Platt, is a frequent speaker and writer on legal
technology issues, with a particular emphasis on Internet issues. *The Lawyer's Quick Guide to Internet E-Mail* clearly and concisely covers the basics
of setting up your e-mail program; sending, receiving, and replying to
e-mail messages; managing the messages you receive; using mailing lists;
sending documents and other files by e-mail; and understanding e-mail

security issues. Informative appendices discuss common error messages, clipping services, virus hoaxes, unsolicited junk e-mail ("spam"), and sources for other e-mail programs and provide a glossary that includes those ubiquitous e-mail abbreviations (such as IMHO, "in my humble opinion") and "smiley face" characters. Also included is a list of additional resources you can access online for further information on general e-mail reference; domain names and Internet service providers; tips on using Eudora, Microsoft Internet Explorer, and Netscape Navigator; "netiquette" rules; address directories; mailing lists; and security and ethics issues.

LPM Publishing is pleased to bring you this highly informative addition to our line of Internet books to assist the practicing lawyer. We trust that you will find it to be a useful adjunct to your practice.

Robert J. Conroy
Judith L. Grubner
Co-Chairs, LPM Publishing

Introduction

As THE INTERNET GROWS, so does the use—and necessity—of e-mail. Most Internet traffic consists of e-mail. Moreover, in the practice of law, e-mail is becoming increasingly important. It's a way of communicating within the firm. It's a way of communicating with clients. It's a way of communicating with other lawyers and getting assistance delivered right to your desktop.

A lawyer who doesn't use e-mail these days is at a competitive disadvantage. Those who do use Internet e-mail—and use it effectively—can increase their client service, their own skills, and their practice. These "by-products" of e-mail are the subject of this book.

Why Internet E-mail?

So what's the deal with Internet e-mail? Why is it so important? Why should you care about using it? E-mail has many significant benefits.

E-mail is a fast way to deliver information. E-mail is much quicker than overnight delivery or "snail mail" (i.e., mail delivered by the post office). Messages can be delivered across the globe in a few seconds to a few hours.

E-mail is virtually free. There is rarely any incremental cost for e-mail if you already use the Internet. Typically the cost is included in your normal Internet or online service monthly fees. Even if you pay by the minute for Internet access, the only charge associated with e-mail is the small amount of connection time to send and receive messages. (You typically read and create messages off-line, when you're not directly connected to the Internet.)

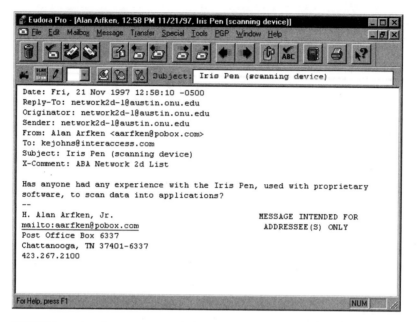

FIGURE I-1. E-mail messages can help you obtain advice from your colleagues. This message was delivered by a legal technology mailing list (discussed in Chapter 6). The e-mail program being used is Eudora Pro 3.0.

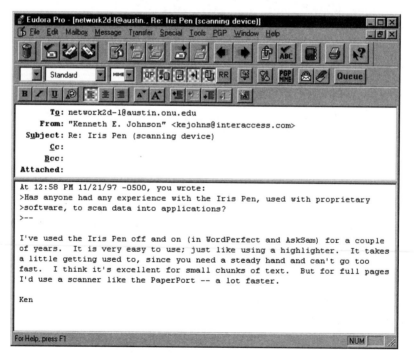

FIGURE I-2. This is a reply to the message shown in Figure I-1. The lines starting with ">" were automatically included from the original message (as explained in Chapter 4). The subject line is prefixed with "Re:" to indicate a reply.

Other files can be sent with e-mail messages. More than just text, e-mail messages can include other files as attachments. Therefore, you can send along documents, graphics, sound and video clips, programs, and the like. (This benefit is discussed in Chapter 7.)

E-mail saves money by reducing other costs. E-mail can help reduce phone charges, since many long-distance calls can be replaced with e-mail messages. Voice messages can also be recorded, attached to an e-mail message, and sent as well. By attaching documents to e-mail, you also reduce the use of faxing and air courier services. In addition, distributing firm publications like newsletters via e-mail saves on postage costs.

Time zones make no difference. You can send e-mail at your convenience, and recipients can read it at their convenience. Send a message to someone in Japan when you leave the office in the evening, and that person receives it in the middle of his or her workday.

E-mail allows rapid turnaround of messages. If you send a message to someone who's connected to the Internet when the message comes in, that person can immediately send back a reply, which you'll then get right away if you're still checking your e-mail. This is true whether you're sending a message to a colleague on the next block or to a client overseas.

You can send messages to many people at once. E-mail allows for multiple recipients, as well as multiple carbon copies and blind carbon copies. This makes it easy to send individual messages and also to deliver firm newsletters, announcements, and other firm administrative items via e-mail. (A special way of sending information to multiple recipients is through a mailing list, discussed in Chapter 6.)

Replying to a message is easy. Click on one button and you can create a reply to a message. Some mail programs allow you to "Reply to All," whereby your reply will also go to other recipients of the original message you received.

Quoting keeps the subject at hand. E-mail programs allow you to include the text of the original message so that recipients can remember what they said in the context of your reply. In a series of replies, this becomes a "thread" that allows you to review the conversation's flow from the beginning.

Messages can be saved in folders and searched electronically. Your e-mail can be categorized and searched later, thus becoming an information repository. Text from messages can be copied and pasted into documents or saved into a firm database.

Phone calls are often screened, but e-mail rarely is. Many people (perhaps you) have a secretary screen phone calls. Rarely, however, does a secretary screen e-mail, so you usually have a direct contact with the recipient.

E-mail extends your deadlines. Perhaps you need to have something at a client's office first thing Monday morning. By using e-mail, you can send it late Sunday evening (or even early Monday morning), and it will be waiting for the client when the client checks for e-mail at the start of the workday.

E-mail can follow you on the road. Regardless of where you are, if you can get on the Internet, you can respond to your e-mail and keep in touch with your office and your clients. If you have a local e-mail account and move to another city and get a new e-mail address, your old mail can usually be automatically forwarded to your new account until everyone knows your new address.

You can have custom-tailored information delivered directly to you. This is sometimes termed "push technology," whereby services send you information, via e-mail, on topics you've specified. For example, West's WESTClip service will automatically e-mail you the results of a Westlaw search on a regular basis.

E-mail improves internal communication in the firm. In a medium- to large-size law firm, you can use e-mail internally for administrative notices and meeting schedules and to get advice from other lawyers. E-mail saves paper and the labor costs of distributing printed material (particularly in a multioffice firm). Distributing mail on an internal e-mail system is almost instantaneous. Everyone gets the information simultaneously.

Are There Drawbacks?

There are some disadvantages that you must be aware of as an e-mail user.

Not everyone has e-mail. Don't assume that everyone with whom you need to communicate has an e-mail address, although the number of users continues to increase rapidly.

Messages can be delayed by computer problems on the Internet. An e-mail message can be delayed if there are problems with a computer that's transporting the message. If the recipient's mail server (the computer that stores that party's e-mail) is down, the recipient cannot receive e-mail messages. However, the Internet network keeps trying to deliver messages. Typically you will receive one or more nondelivery notifications, indicating a problem. The vast majority of e-mail eventually goes through.

Messages aren't really "received" until the recipient checks for e-mail. A message can sit on someone's mail server for any length of time. Until recipients check their mail and transfer a message to their e-mail program, where it can be read, they won't know the message is there.

Return receipts are practically nonexistent. Although some e-mail programs let you specify a return receipt, few mail systems currently support this feature over the Internet.

Received mail doesn't equal read mail. Just because a message was received by someone doesn't mean that person has read it. Most people get many e-mail messages each day and often don't read all their messages at once. Once a message is transferred into the recipient's mail program, it may be many hours before it's actually read.

E-mail isn't private. Don't assume that only the recipient of the message can read it. If security is a concern, messages can be encrypted so that only the recipient can "decode" and read them (as discussed in Chapter 8). For practical purposes, though, e-mail should be considered as secure as many other common means of communication, such as phone calls, faxes, the U.S. mail, and express delivery services.

E-mail is not designed for immediacy. Not everyone is online checking their mail all the time. If you send an e-mail message to several people requesting a conference call in one hour, chances are that not all the parties will read their mail within that sixty minutes. (That antique on your desk called a telephone is better for urgent communication.) If, however, you send an e-mail message about a conference call in two days, it is likely that most of the recipients will read it in time to participate.

It's easy to miss tone in e-mail. One advantage of a phone conversation is that you can pick up on verbal cues like tone, inflection, sarcasm, and so forth. These are very difficult to convey in writing, so it's easy for what you're saying to be misinterpreted in an e-mail message. (There are, however, ways to tip off the reader to your tone, as discussed in Chapter 3.)

Changing your e-mail address may be complicated. E-mail doesn't necessarily follow you when you change your e-mail address. If you have your mail at one Internet service provider and then switch to another (or switch from an online service to an Internet service provider), your e-mail is not always forwarded from the original address.

On the whole, the advantages of e-mail outweigh the disadvantages, though you need to keep the latter points in mind as you send and receive messages. However, I haven't explicitly mentioned the most important reason for using e-mail.

Your Clients Want to Send E-mail to You

The best reason for using e-mail is that it's what your clients want. Many clients are now requiring e-mail access to their lawyers. It's for many of the same reasons discussed earlier. E-mail allows rapid, low-cost delivery of messages. Messages can be immediately responded to, particularly if both the client and law firm have full-time Internet access and delivery of e-mail. E-mail messages can easily be sent to different individuals at the same client company, or to different lawyers at the same firm, even if they are in different locations. Co-counsel can readily be copied on messages relating to a particular matter.

Clients know that e-mail can avoid telephone tag, or going through a secretary on every phone call. Moreover, clients can stay in touch when they are traveling, whether it be by carrying a laptop or by using a computer where they are staying. If you can get on the Internet, you can get your e-mail (as explained in Chapter 5). Just as if they were in the office, clients can review documents that you send via attachment to the mail message.

In addition, many clients and potential clients like the immediacy of newsletters and other legal information distributed by e-mail. For example, Siskind, Susser, Haas & Chang's World Wide Web site (**http://www. visalaw.com**) offers registration for its Immigration Bulletin, delivered by e-mail.

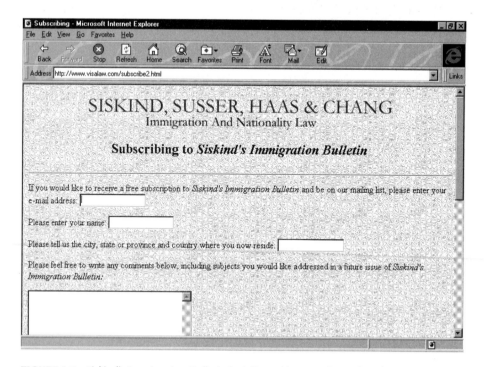

FIGURE I-3. Siskind's Immigration Bulletin is delivered by e-mail to subscribers who register on the firm's Web site.

About This Book

This book is intended to give readers a quick and easy introduction to Internet e-mail and how to use it effectively. Most of the topics discussed are applicable to any e-mail program, though some programs offer more features (like filtering) than others. We'll concentrate on three major e-mail programs:

- Eudora®, from Qualcomm, is one of the most popular e-mail programs on the market. Eudora is available in a retail version (Pro) and a free version (Light), which can be downloaded from the World Wide Web.
- Netscape® Messenger is the e-mail component of Netscape® Communicator and the Netscape Navigator® Web browser.
- Microsoft® Outlook Express is the e-mail component of Microsoft® Internet Explorer.

Why choose these programs? Eudora was chosen because of its power and popularity. Netscape Messenger and Microsoft Outlook Express come with the browser and are likely on your computer already—and so, in essence, are "free."

Although the book focuses on these three programs, many of the e-mail features discussed are applicable to other mail programs. However, some features may be missing in your e-mail software. For example, some e-mail systems don't allow blind carbon copies (discussed in Chapter 3), and others don't support quoting (discussed in Chapter 4). Nonetheless, most of the features covered are common to current versions of Internet e-mail software.

The book is organized to take you through the basics of setting up your e-mail program, sending messages, receiving and replying to e-mail, and managing the messages you receive. It then moves on to more intermediate topics, such as using mailing lists, sending documents (and other files) by e-mail, and understanding the security aspects of using e-mail. The first appendix covers a few more-advanced topics, like mail errors, the potential for viruses, and junk e-mail. The book ends with an e-mail glossary, which explains all of those three-letter acronyms in your messages, and a directory of online resources for e-mail and e-mail software.

CHAPTER **ONE**

E-mail Basics

To BECOME AN INTERNET E-MAIL USER, you must have two things: an e-mail account from which to send and receive mail and an e-mail program to create and read messages.

Getting an E-mail Account

If your firm currently has an internal e-mail program, you can probably use it to send and receive Internet mail. Check with your computer services staff. Internal e-mail systems, such as cc:Mail or Microsoft Mail, often use a "gateway" to the Internet. A gateway is a computer system that transfers data, like e-mail, between two normally incompatible networks, converting the data so that each network understands it. On one side is the Internet, and on the other is your firm's e-mail system.

If your firm doesn't have an internal e-mail system, or if you want to have a personal account to send and receive messages, you have the option of getting Internet mail through an Internet service provider (ISP) or through an online service such as America Online (AOL) or CompuServe (or both, since it is common for people to have multiple mail accounts). In deciding where your mail will be, you need to consider several factors.

First, ISPs usually provide e-mail software (and assistance) when you establish your account. The software is often Eudora Light, the free version of Eudora. However, you can use any Internet e-mail program that will work with the ISP's mail services.

Commercial services, on the other hand, generally require that you use their software with their e-mail system. Both AOL and CompuServe have their own mail programs, which don't have as many features as the Internet mail programs discussed herein. Although this is likely to change in the future, currently you must use the services' programs to access your e-mail on those services.

Another factor to consider is that commercial services have many local telephone access numbers. Consequently, if you travel extensively, checking your e-mail often involves only a local call. While some ISPs are national, most are local, so dialing in for your mail could involve a long-distance call, though likely a short one.

Lastly, ISPs offer "domain name" services, so mail can be addressed to your firm. If you are a solo or small firm practitioner, you may want to establish a domain name where you can receive e-mail. A domain name is like a vanity address on the Internet—it's where your mail is addressed (as discussed in the next chapter) and where your Web site is located (if you have one). From a technical perspective, a domain name identifies a unique computer on the Internet. My firm's domain name is mayerbrown.com, with e-mail being addressed to an individual at that domain (e.g., kejohnson@mayerbrown.com). Without a domain name, your e-mail address will carry the domain name of your online service (e.g., johnson265@aol.com) or ISP (e.g., kejohns@interaccess.com). Some clients see a domain name as being more professional, and an address at an online service as akin to having a "c/o" on your business card.

Finding an ISP

ISPs have sprung up all over, from mom-and-pop shops to national ISPs such as Netcom and PSINet. There are several ways of finding an ISP for your mail service:

- Check with colleagues and firm staff for recommendations.
- Bar associations, chambers of commerce, and computer user groups often have special group discounts with an ISP. If you're a member of such an organization, the ISP has already been prescreened for you.
- Local ISPs frequently advertise in the business section of your newspaper and in local computer newsletters and magazines.
- On the World Wide Web, you can quickly find ISPs in your area by checking out "The List" at http://thelist.iworld.com. You can search for ISPs by name, geographic area, and area code. The site contains "links" to the ISPs listed, so you can jump to specific information about that company.

Once you find a prospective ISP, you'll want to ask some questions:

1. What kind of account does the ISP offer? You want to look for a PPP account, PPP being an acronym for Point-to-Point Protocol. PPP is one of the standards for directly connecting a computer to the Internet through telephone lines. The other, and older, standard is SLIP, for Serial Line Internet Protocol.
2. What are the prices for service? This includes initial setup charges, monthly rates, hourly rates, storage charges, and so forth. Are there any surcharges, such as for dialing in during business hours or taking up more than a certain amount of storage space?
3. What are the phone numbers? Are there enough local numbers in your area to ensure that dialing in will mean a local call? If you're traveling, are there toll-free numbers or numbers in other cities to use?
4. Does the ISP provide software, such as an e-mail program or a Web browser, or do you need to obtain these on your own?
5. What are the technical support policies and hours of service? Is there someone you can reach on the phone Sunday night if you can't get your mail off the server? Can you get noncritical support via e-mail and on the ISP's Web site?
6. Does the ISP support the latest 56K high-speed modems?
7. How fast is *its* connection to the Internet? The ISP should have a high-speed trunk line called a T1 line, or the even faster T3, not a modem-based connection.

Generally your best bet is to telephone the ISP and talk to the sales department. The ISP's Web site will usually offer only the most basic information about its service. Ask that its terms of service be sent to you, along with an application for an account.

The focus in this book is on e-mailing through an ISP, using standard e-mail software that will work with any PPP or SLIP e-mail account.

Choosing an E-mail Program

Most current e-mail programs have similar standard features, including the following capabilities:

- Storing names and e-mail addresses through an Address Book feature
- Replying with the text of the original message (called "quoting")

- Storing sent messages
- Forwarding messages
- Saving messages in folders
- Filtering messages (i.e., examining part of the message and performing some action based on what is found there)
- Attaching files to messages

Specific e-mail programs implement these features differently. For example, Eudora can filter incoming and outgoing messages, but Netscape Messenger and Microsoft Outlook Express can only filter messages that you receive. Eudora shows quoted text with a greater than sign (>) before each line, but Netscape Messenger can also show the quoted text in italics and a different color.

The following are among the most popular e-mail programs:

- **Eudora®**. A very popular e-mail program, Eudora is available for Windows 3.1, Windows 95, and the Macintosh. Eudora comes in a commercial package called Eudora Pro and in a free version called Eudora Light. Eudora Light is available at no cost from many ISPs

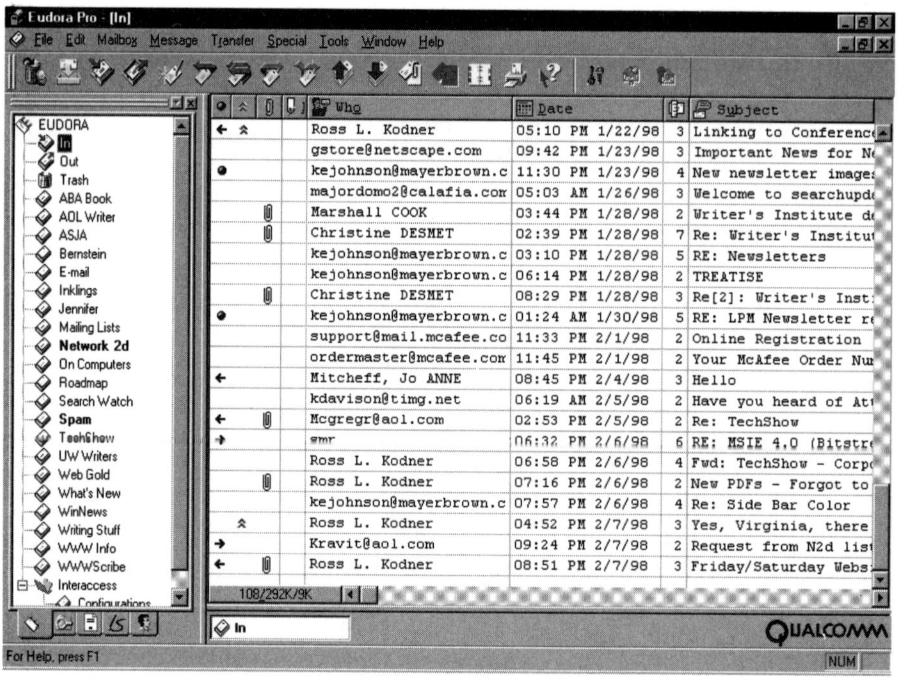

FIGURE 1-1. Eudora Pro 4.0's Inbox. Message folders are optionally displayed at the left of the screen.

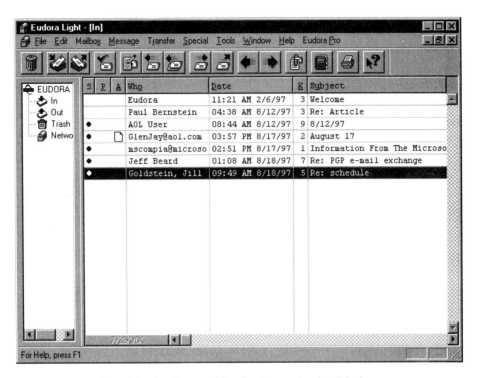

FIGURE 1-2. Eudora Light closely resembles the Pro version, but it lacks some more advanced features such as spelling checking, enhanced filters, and templates for automatic responses.

or by downloading it from Qualcomm's Web site. (See Appendix B for information on where to download e mail software.)

♦ **Netscape® Messenger.** Version 4 of Netscape's Web browser, Netscape Communicator, includes an integrated e-mail program called Netscape Messenger.

♦ **Netscape® Mail.** A less-sophisticated mail program, Netscape Mail is available as part of the Netscape Navigator 2.0 and 3.0 browsers.

♦ **Microsoft® Outlook Express.** Outlook Express is an optional part of the Microsoft Internet Explorer 4.0 Web browser. It can be installed at the same time as the browser or downloaded and installed later. (Internet Explorer 4.0 must be loaded onto your system to download Outlook Express.)

♦ **Microsoft® Internet Mail.** Microsoft's Internet Mail is an optional part of the Internet Explorer 3.0 Web browser.

♦ **Microsoft® Exchange.** Windows 95 users can send and receive Internet mail with Microsoft Exchange, which provides the "Inbox" on your desktop.

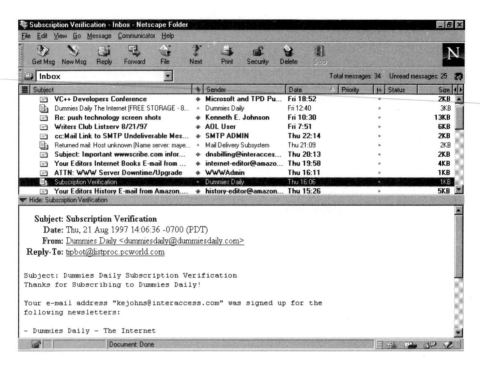

FIGURE 1-3. Netscape Messenger is the e-mail component of the Netscape Communicator 4.0 package.

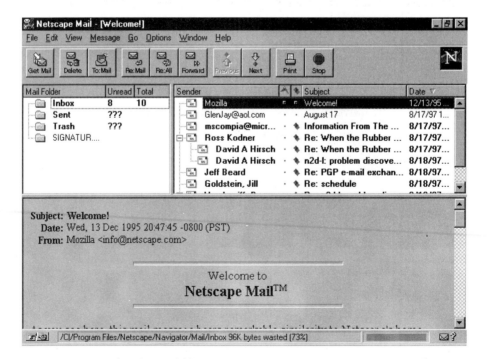

FIGURE 1-4. E-mail is also available in Netscape Navigator 3.0 using Netscape Mail.

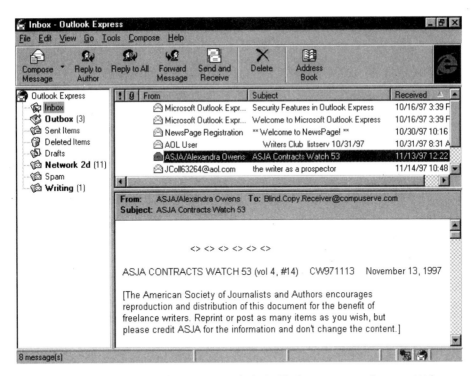

FIGURE 1-5. Microsoft Outlook Express is included with the Internet Explorer 4.0 Web browser, available free from Microsoft.

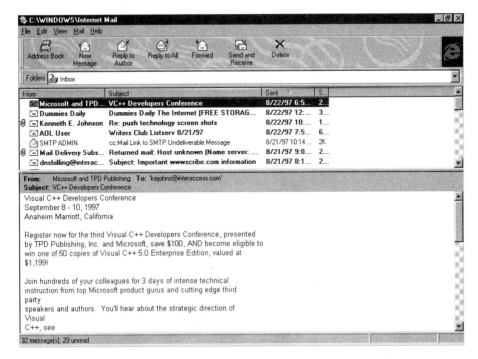

FIGURE 1-6. Internet Mail and News is an optional component of Microsoft Internet Explorer 3.0.

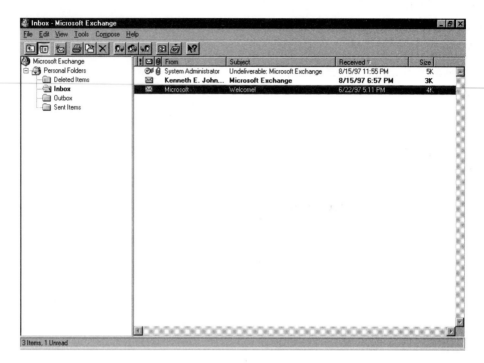

FIGURE 1-7. For Windows 95 users, Internet mail capabilities are provided under Microsoft Exchange.

Using Web-Based E-mail

A new alternative is Web-based e-mail, in which you use your browser to send and receive mail through a particular Web site. One such site is Yahoo Mail (http://mail.yahoo.com). Your mail account is free because the site is supported by customized advertising that you receive after registering and completing a user profile. The advantage of Yahoo Mail is that you can access it from any computer that has a Web browser. No software configurations are required on your part.

Web-based mail can be a money saver for a firm because each lawyer can have an e-mail address without having a separate Internet account (which, with most ISPs, runs about twenty dollars a month). The firm can have one dial-up Internet account for everyone's use. Once connected, each lawyer can check his or her mail with the Web browser. However, if this is done from shared computers, there may be some e-mail security concerns (an aspect discussed in Chapters 5 and 8).

Note that sources for Web-based e-mail are expanding. Many Web search engines sites, such as Yahoo (http://mail.yahoo.com), are now offering customer e-mail addresses.

How E-mail Works

Internet e-mail is a store-and-forward service. Like the Internet itself, the computer sending the mail and the computer receiving the mail do not need to be directly connected. The mail is passed from one computer to another until it reaches its destination. Each of the intermediary computers temporarily stores the message before sending it on to the next computer.

It's not even necessary that the source and destination computers both be on the Internet. Computer gateways connect different and incompatible networks, such as the Internet and a client's internal network and e-mail system. These gateways know how to reformat messages from one network so that they are readable on the other.

A computer system handles e-mail through a "daemon." A daemon is a program running in the background, waiting to perform some function. When certain conditions are met, the program performs its function without any human intervention. When an e-mail message arrives, the daemon checks to see if the recipient is on that computer system. If so, the daemon delivers the message; if not, it forwards the message on to another computer system that may have that recipient, and that system's daemon examines the message. If the recipient is on that system, then the message is moved into the individual's Inbox; if not, it is forwarded on to another computer system. This continues until the message is delivered.

This may all sound very inefficient, but actually it's very practical. If there was only one connection between the sender and receiver, and that connection went bad, the mail couldn't get through. By having multiple paths between any two computers on the network, there are usually alternative connections available if trouble is encountered. This is the basic architecture of the Internet, which was developed during the Cold War to provide reliable military and government communications in case of nuclear war.

How Gateways Function

As previously mentioned, a gateway is a special type of computer that connects different computer systems that normally could not communicate. E-mail gateways link Internet mail services with a proprietary mail program, reformatting messages so that e-mail users on each side of the connection can read messages from the other side. For example, when e-mail messages are sent to AOL subscribers through the Internet, an AOL e-mail gateway converts the Internet messages to the mail format used by AOL (and vice versa when AOL users send e-mail to Internet addresses).

Gateways also integrate a firm's network-based e-mail system into the Internet. For example, my firm uses Lotus cc:Mail. In and of itself, cc:Mail cannot send messages through the Internet. With a gateway, however, sending mail to a client at an Internet address is as easy as sending mail to the managing partner down the hall. If it has a gateway installed, your firm's e-mail system can also serve as an Internet mail package. Most network e-mail vendors offer gateways as part of their base package or as a separate purchase.

Communicating through Protocols

When you are ready to send or receive e-mail, you log on to the Internet through your ISP. Your e-mail program communicates with the mail server at the ISP through "protocols," which are simply definitions of how computers talk to one another. Standard protocols allow different computers and computers with different operating systems and software to communicate reliably, since they all speak the same "language." So, for example, a law firm that uses Windows 95 can send e-mail to a client who uses an Apple Macintosh, and the client can reply to the firm—with no conversion required on either side.

Your e-mail program uses two protocols: the Post Office Protocol, commonly referred to as POP or POP3, and the Simple Mail Transfer Protocol, commonly known as SMTP. POP, or POP3, handles e-mail downloads from the mail server to your computer. SMTP transfers messages from one system to another on the Internet. You'll see references to these when you're configuring your e-mail program for the first time, as discussed in the next chapter.

CHAPTER TWO

Setting Up Your E-mail Program

AFTER ESTABLISHING AN ACCOUNT WITH AN ISP and choosing an e-mail program, the next step is installing and configuring your e-mail software.

Your E-mail Program's Main Screen

E-mail programs typically open with the Inbox displayed on the screen. There is a menu bar along with a toolbar with icons for common mail activities. You may also see a list of folders (in Eudora and Outlook Express) as well as a preview window showing the contents of whatever message is highlighted (in Netscape Messenger, Outlook Express, and Eudora Pro 4.0). In fact, these programs give you a good deal of control over how the screen looks, from what is displayed to the toolbar buttons used. For example, you can usually choose what information to see about each message (e.g., sender, date received, priority, and attachments); the order in which these columns are displayed; whether to view the mailbox folders where stored messages are kept; whether to display a message preview window; and what toolbar buttons are used. Customizing your e-mail to work exactly as you work is easy.

Eudora Pro starts with the Inbox open and a list of mailboxes in a pane on the left of the screen. These mailboxes correspond to the folders

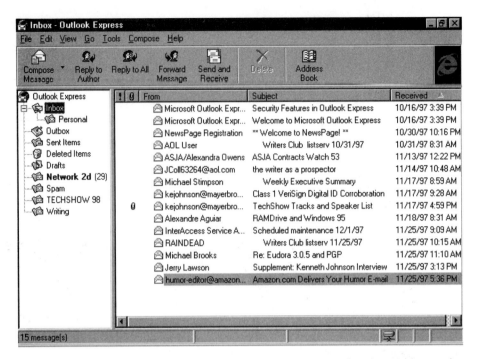

FIGURE 2-1. Microsoft Outlook Express's screen has been configured to show folders on the left of the screen and not to display the preview window. The message columns are set to show (in order) priority, attachments, sender, subject, and date received.

in Netscape's and Microsoft's mail programs. Mailboxes with unread messages are displayed in bold. The mailbox columns indicate message status, priority, attachments (with a page or paper clip icon indicating an attached file), sender, date, size (in kilobytes), and subject.

In Eudora Pro 4.0, at the bottom of the mailbox pane, there are tabs for other functions. These include File Browser (where files can be attached to messages by dragging them), Stationery (for template messages), Signature (for text appended to the end of each message), and Personalities (for settings for multiple e-mail accounts).

Netscape Messenger's main screen starts in the Inbox. You can go to different folders by clicking on the down arrow next to the folder name, just under the toolbar. A preview pane at the bottom of the screen displays whatever message is highlighted. In each folder the columns show message subject, sender, date, and priority, with additional fields such as status and size available by scrolling to the right. Unread messages display with a closed envelope icon, in bold, and with a green triangle in a column between subject and sender.

Microsoft Outlook Express's main screen is a combination of the Eudora and Netscape Messenger formats, showing folders on the left, the In-

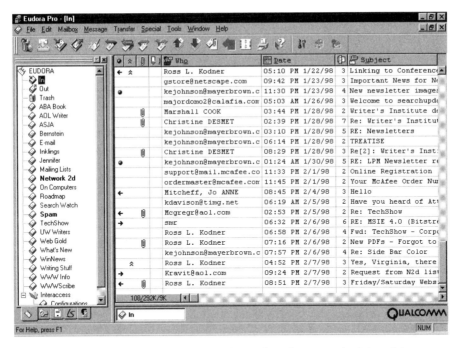

FIGURE 2-2. Eudora's main screen displays a list of all mailboxes on the left and the contents of the selected mailbox on the right. In version 4.0, tabs at the bottom of the mailbox pane correspond to the Mailboxes, File Browser, Stationery, Signature, and Personalities features.

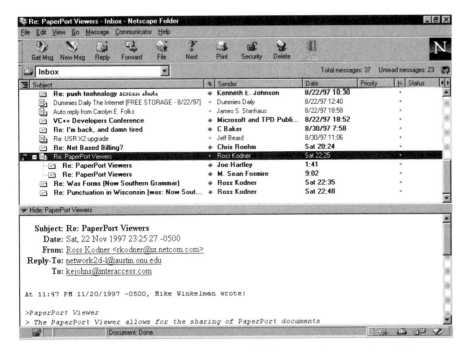

FIGURE 2-3. Netscape Messenger's main screen includes a preview pane that displays messages in the bottom half of the screen. Here Inbox messages are shown in thread order, in which messages and their replies appear together.

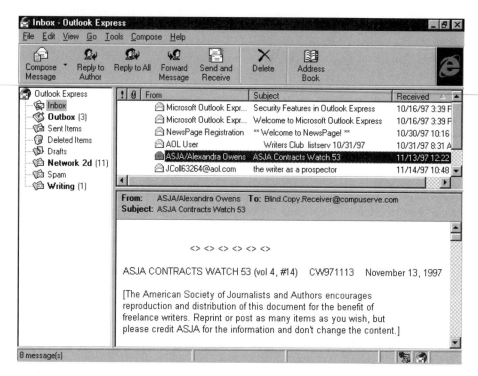

FIGURE 2-4. Microsoft Outlook Express's main screen includes a folders list and preview pane. Both can be turned off so that the message list fills the full screen.

box on the right, and a preview pane below (which can also be shown vertically). Folders with unread messages are displayed in bold, with the number of those messages shown in parentheses. Unread messages in each folder are also displayed in bold. Folder columns indicate message priority, attachments, sender, subject, and date received.

The Menu Bar

The menu bar provides access to all the options needed to use the program. Although Eudora, Netscape Messenger, and Microsoft Outlook Express have common functionality, getting to those functions generally involves different menu selections. These are four common menu selections:

- **File:** For performing common file activities like creating new messages, saving a message in a file, getting new messages, printing messages, and exiting the program.

- **Edit:** For editing functions such as cutting, copying, and pasting text, formatting text in the message, finding text or messages, and spelling checking.
- **Message** (in Eudora and Netscape Messenger) or **Compose** (in Outlook Express): For message options like creating new messages, changing message priority, and replying or forwarding messages.
- **Help:** For accessing help on the program.

Luckily, your most common activities when using e-mail are only a mouse-click away on the toolbar.

The Toolbar

The toolbar, sometimes called an icon bar, appears below the menu bar and contains commonly used commands. Its buttons display distinctive icons and sometimes text. Both Eudora and Outlook Express let you customize the toolbar by adding new buttons or rearranging their order. A button's appearance may change (e.g., become "dimmed out" and not selectable) when that command is not available. Additional buttons will display when sending, replying, or forwarding a message.

In Eudora
Eudora's standard toolbar includes commands for the following:

- Delete the message
- Connect to the Internet to check for new mail and send any waiting messages
- Open the Inbox

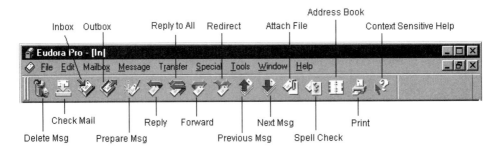

FIGURE 2-5. Eudora's standard toolbar.

- Open the Outbox (which contains messages waiting to be sent, as well as all those sent)
- Prepare a new message
- Reply to a message
- Reply to all (meaning all addresses in the original message are included in the reply)
- Forward the message
- Redirect the message (meaning to send the message to someone else, as though coming from the original sender)
- Read the previous message
- Read the next message
- Attach a file to the message
- Spell check the message
- Open the Address Book
- Print the message
- Context sensitive help

Eudora's toolbar expands downward when you are sending (or replying to or forwarding) a message. The toolbar's middle section has message options, many of which you don't have to change from the defaults. Among the other buttons are these:

- Priority of the message
- Signature to use (discussed later)
- Encoding method for attachments (covered in Chapter 7)
- Return receipt

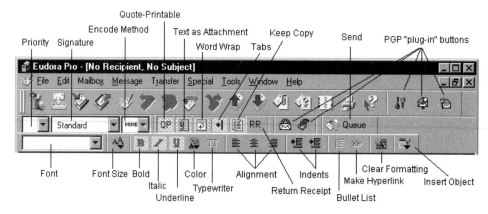

FIGURE 2-6. When sending a message, Eudora Pro's toolbar expands to include text formatting and messaging options. The PGP buttons are from PGP for Personal Privacy (a separate security program discussed in Chapter 8).

◆ Send/Queue the message (with queue meaning that you will explicitly tell Eudora to send the message later, and meanwhile it is to be
stored in the Outbox)

If you have any "plug-ins" installed with Eudora, their buttons will
also display on the toolbar. Plug-ins are special add-on programs that provide additional functionality. For example, PGP for Personal Privacy for
Eudora (discussed in Chapter 8) is a plug-in for encrypting messages.
When installed, clicking on its button will encrypt the message when
sent.

The bottom third of the Eudora expanded toolbar contains message
formatting buttons. The formatting options include bold, underline, italics, colors, font size, line justification, and indents. These are relevant
only if you send e-mail in a special format called HyperText Markup Language (HTML) or text-enriched (as discussed in Chapter 3). Normal, plain-
text messages cannot carry these types of text formatting. (By the way,
you cannot customize the buttons that appear on the second and third
rows of the expanded toolbar.)

In Netscape Messenger

Netscape Messenger's standard toolbar includes both message and e-mail
transmission options for the following:

◆ Connect to the Internet to get new mail (and send any waiting
messages)
◆ Create a new message
◆ Reply to a message/Reply to all
◆ Forward the message
◆ File the message (i.e., store it in a folder)

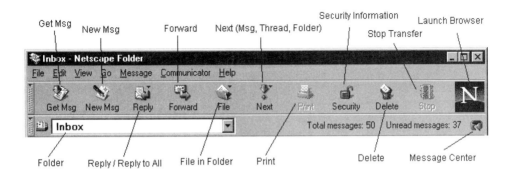

FIGURE 2-7. Netscape Messenger's standard toolbar.

- Next message option (includes the next message, next unread message, next flagged message, next unread thread, next folder, and next unread folder)
- Print the message
- Security information (i.e., general Netscape Communicator security information and specific security details on an opened message)
- Delete the message
- Stop the mail transfer
- Launch the Netscape Navigator browser

Below the primary toolbar buttons is a folders list, where you click on the down arrow and select the folder you want to view. At the right is a green arrow for displaying the Message Center, which is a separate window showing all your folders and the count of read and unread messages in each. It corresponds to Eudora's mailbox list and Outlook Express's folders list.

Unlike Eudora, which expands the existing toolbar when you're creating a message, Netscape Messenger displays a new toolbar with only those features used for sending messages. These include the following:

- Send the message
- Quote the previous message (meaning that if you have quoting turned off and want to include the text from the message to which you're replying, this button will bring it in)
- Address the message from the Address Book
- Attach a file, a Web page, or your address card (discussed later)
- Spell check the message
- Save the message as a draft, to be completed later
- Specify the security settings for the message

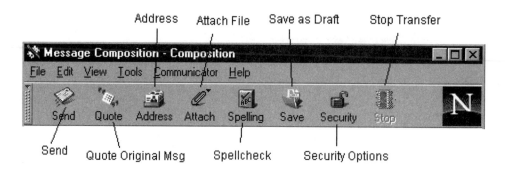

FIGURE 2-8. When sending a message, Netscape Messenger's toolbar displays buttons for sending, quoting, addressing, and securing the message.

◆ Stop the message transfer

Additional sending options appear below the toolbar, on a tab within the addressing section of the message. Here you can set the method for attaching files, specify return receipt and message priority, and indicate whether to use plain text or HTML format in the message.

In Microsoft Outlook Express

Lastly, there is Microsoft Outlook Express's toolbar, which contains the following options:

◆ Create a new message
◆ Create a new message using stationery (i.e., preformatted message styles with themed graphics, such as for birthday greetings)
◆ Reply to the message
◆ Reply to all
◆ Forward the message
◆ Connect to the Internet to send and receive e-mail
◆ Delete the message
◆ Open the Address Book
◆ Launch the Internet Explorer Web browser

When you are working on a message, Outlook Express's toolbar changes to display the following options:

◆ Send the message
◆ Undo the last edit
◆ Cut, copy, or paste text from the clipboard

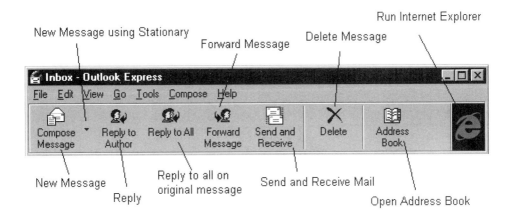

FIGURE 2-9. Microsoft Outlook Express's standard toolbar.

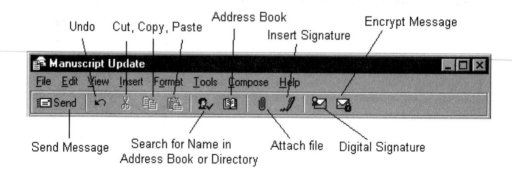

FIGURE 2-10. Outlook Express's toolbar changes to include specific editing functions when you are working on a message.

- Search for a name in the Address Book
- Open the Address Book
- Attach a file
- Add your signature to the message
- Digitally sign the message (discussed in Chapter 8)
- Encrypt the message (also discussed in Chapter 8)

A Tour of Your Mailboxes

Your e-mail program has several different folders, or mailboxes. (They're called mailboxes in Eudora and folders in Netscape Messenger and Outlook Express.) You can create new folders or mailboxes at any time to store messages. There are also some standard ones.

The Inbox holds your incoming messages. For each message, it displays the sender, the subject, the date and time the message was sent, and whether the message is read or unread. The Outbox/Unsent Messages contains messages to be sent. In Eudora, the Outbox also contains sent messages. Sent Items, in both Netscape Messenger and Microsoft Outlook Express, is a separate folder for messages that have been successfully sent. In both programs, the Outbox holds only messages not yet sent or those not sent successfully.

Deleted messages are moved to the Trash/Deleted Items folder. You can choose to remove these messages manually or else automatically when exiting the e-mail program.

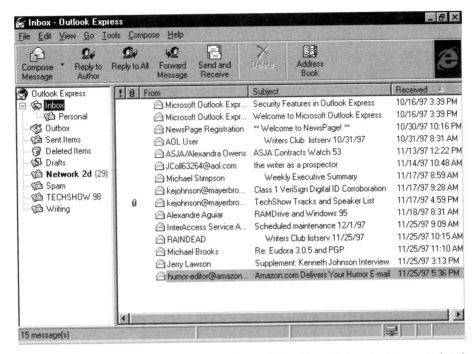

FIGURE 2-11. Outlook Express's standard folders include Inbox, Outbox, Sent Items, Deleted Items, and Drafts. Additional folders can be created to organize your mail. The numbers by the folders indicate the number of unread messages.

In addition, in Netscape Messenger and Microsoft Outlook Express, the Drafts folder contains draft messages that are not yet ready to be sent. Eudora does not have a Drafts mailbox.

Your E-mail Address

Everyone who uses Internet mail has a unique address consisting of two parts: (1) their user name and (2) the name of the network where they receive their mail, called the domain. These two parts are connected by an @ sign, as in this address:

> **kejohns@interaccess.com** (kejohns = user name, interaccess.com = domain)

or

> **70530.1677@compuserve.com** (70530.1677= user name, compuserve.com = domain)

The user name is the mailbox for the person on the domain computer; each user on that domain must have a unique name. (It may or may not be related to the person's "real" name.) Domain names help computer networks keep track of one another because a domain name identifies a specific computer on the Internet. Since the domain must be unique to each computer and the user name unique for each person on that domain, no two people can have the same e-mail address. The user name and the domain can contain letters, numbers, and some punctuation like underscores or periods. An e-mail address cannot contain spaces or commas. Note that addresses are traditionally given in lowercase.

The domain name often conveys geographic and functional information about who owns and operates the domain. A full domain name looks like this:

subdomain.domain.type

or

subdomain.domain.type.where

"Subdomain" means the smallest unit of the domain name. It usually represents a single computer or a small network within the larger domain network. Some e-mail addresses will contain subdomains, and some will not. "Type" means the top level of the domain name, which identifies the broad function of that network. Top-level organizational domains include the following:

- **com:** Originally intended for commercial entities.
- **edu:** Originally designated for four-year, degree-granting colleges and universities, but now used for a variety of educational institutions.
- **gov:** Used for agencies and branches of the U.S. federal government.
- **mil:** Used for U.S. military entities.
- **net:** Designated for entities and computers that are part of the Internet's infrastructure, such as networking organizations.
- **org:** Used for miscellaneous entities that do not fit under any of the other top-level domains, often not-for-profit groups.

Discussions are currently under way to add additional top-level domains, because we are rapidly running out of domain names. Of interest to lawyers are the potential domains of **.law, .firm,** or **.lawfirm.**

Some domain names include a "where" suffix, which appears after the domain type. This is a country code, representing the country of the domain computer. Examples include **.us** for the United States, **.ca** for Canada, **.mx** for Mexico, and **.uk** for the United Kingdom.

My Internet address at my firm is

kejohnson@mayerbrown.com

My user name is "kejohnson" on this computer, with "mayerbrown" being the domain (there is no subdomain) and "com" identifying this as a commercial domain. The "where" (.us) is not used.

One important fact to remember is that people often have multiple e-mail accounts and multiple e-mail addresses. It's important to know which one to use because the person to whom you're sending mail may not check all of his or her e-mail accounts regularly. For example, you could reach me at all of the following:

kejohnson@mayerbrown.com (my work account)
kejohnson@interaccess.com (my personal account)
kenj@wwwscribe.com (my Web site)
info@wwwscribe.com (also my Web site)
kjohnson@oncomputers.com (an account from a writing assignment)
ken_johnson@rocketmail.com (a Web-based e-mail account)
InternetScribe@yahoo.com (another Web-based e-mail account)
70530.1677@compuserve.com (my CompuServe account)
johnson265@aol.com (my America Online account)

One note about CompuServe addresses: Most CompuServe user accounts use a series of numbers, separated by a comma (e.g., 70530,1677). Since commas aren't allowed in e-mail addresses, when sending Internet mail to a CompuServe user, you must replace the comma with a period (e.g., 70530.1677). CompuServe now allows users to have a "real name" address, so we'll likely be seeing less of the numeric addresses in the future.

My kenj@wwwscribe.com address illustrates another aspect of e-mail addresses—they don't have to be a real mail account. In my case, kenj@wwwscribe.com is "aliased" to my kejohns@interaccess.com account. Any mail sent to kenj@wwwscribe.com will automatically be directed to my InterAccess mailbox, without the sender being aware of it.

Aliasing means that once you have an e-mail account, you can create additional e-mail addresses for specific purposes that are aliased to that account. For example, these addresses can point to different departments, positions, or practice areas in the firm:

library@lawfirm.com
managing.partner@lawfirm.com

bankruptcy@lawfirm.com
recruiting@lawfirm.com
summer_associates@lawfirm.com

Aliasing is also a way that a firm's offices in different cities can share the same aliased domain even if each office uses a different ISP and different mail servers. In the case of Chicago lawyer Tom Jones and Atlanta lawyer Mary Smith, their addresses could be

tjones@lawfirm.com
msmith@lawfirm.com

Jones's mail could be directed to the firm's ISP in Chicago and Smith's mail to the firm's ISP in Atlanta.

With more people getting Internet e-mail and having multiple addresses, the big question is: How do you find a particular person's e-mail address?

How to Find E-mail Addresses

The surest way to find someone's e-mail address is to *ask* the person! In our technological world there's often a reluctance to use an old technology like picking up the phone and calling someone, but it's often the best way to get an e-mail address.

In addition, e-mail addresses are becoming more common on business cards, stationery, and Web sites. One trick to finding an e-mail address is to find the person's personal Web site, or his or her firm's Web site, and to look for an e-mail link. This is a special type of hypertext link that, when you click on it, opens an e-mail window in your browser with the person's e-mail address already entered in the To field.

The Web also includes several sites where you can look up e-mail addresses, including Yahoo White Pages (http://yahoo.four11.com), Bigfoot (http://www.bigfoot.com), and Internet @ddress.finder (http://www.iaf.net). These services' information, however, is far from complete, and it's easy to be swamped with addresses that aren't the one for which you're looking.

One generally frowned upon way of finding someone's e-mail address is to ask the "postmaster" at the person's domain. The postmaster is a special mail account for the individual responsible for the mail system at that domain. Postmasters are typically overworked folks, and they don't necessarily have the time to answer an e-mail asking, "Does Mary Jones have an e-mail account there?" You should contact the postmaster

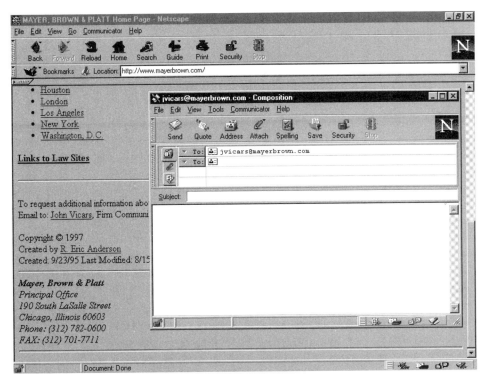

FIGURE 2-12. Many Web pages include a "mailto" link that allows you to send an e-mail message from the Web browser.

(**postmaster@domain**) if you start getting error messages from the domain or to report abuse of an e-mail account there (as discussed in Appendix A).

How to Configure Your E-mail Program

Before you use your e-mail program for the first time, you need to configure it for your mail account. These settings are usually under an Options or Preferences menu, where you identify yourself and, most importantly, indicate the mail server used to send and receive e-mail. You will need to make two mail server entries. Your ISP will give you the information for these when you establish your account:

- ◆ **POP or POP3 account/Incoming mail server:** This protocol handles connecting to the mail server and the downloading of new mail. POP3 is the current version.
- ◆ **SMTP account/Outgoing mail server:** This protocol handles the actual sending of mail through the Internet.

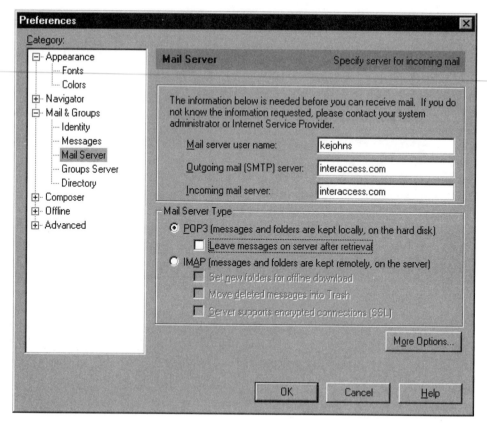

FIGURE 2-13. With Netscape Messenger, the incoming and outgoing mail servers are specified under the Mail Server Preferences menu. Here you can also indicate whether to keep messages on the server after downloading them to Messenger.

In addition to the mail servers, there are other configuration options to set:

- **Real name:** Your given name, which is included with your e-mail address on messages that you send. This name will appear in the From or Sender field in the recipient's Inbox, making it a little more obvious who the message is from (i.e., "Kenneth E. Johnson" as opposed to "kejohns@interaccess.com").
- **Reply to address** (if different from your e-mail address): This is where the mail will go when the recipient clicks on the reply button for your message.
- **Organization:** The organization's name, such as the title of your law firm. This appears in the header of messages you send.

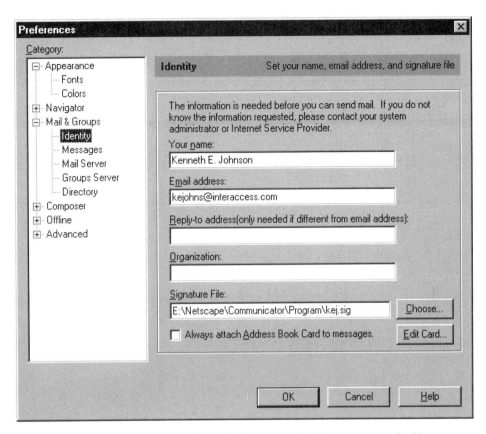

FIGURE 2-14. Netscape Messenger's Identity Preferences include name, e-mail address, organization, and signature file.

- **Signature text:** The text to be appended to each message you send.
- **Leave mail on server:** Whether to delete messages from the mail server after they are transferred to your mail program. Typically you want to set this to "yes" to delete, unless you plan to check your mail from more than one computer (an option discussed in Chapter 5).

If the password is not previously entered, your e-mail program will ask for your POP account password the first time you check for mail. Most programs offer to "remember" the password so you do not have to enter it each time. While convenient, this is also a security risk if someone else uses your computer. Laptop users in particular should leave the password blank, in case the laptop is stolen.

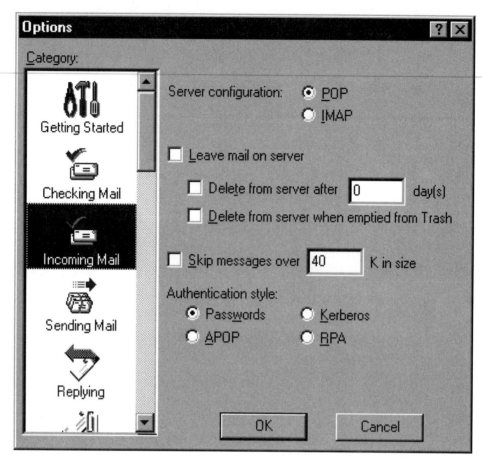

FIGURE 2-15. Eudora's Incoming Mail Options include whether to leave mail on the server after transferring the messages to your program and, if so, whether to delete those messages from the server after a number of days or when emptied from Eudora's Trash.

Configuring Multiple Accounts

Both Eudora and Outlook Express allow users to configure multiple e-mail accounts, which can be very helpful if you have more than one account that you need to check regularly. By configuring your e-mail program for your multiple accounts, you can check each account during one connection to the Internet.

In Outlook Express you set up multiple accounts by pulling down the Tools menu and selecting Account, then going to the Mail tab and selecting New. In Eudora multiple accounts are called Personalities. With Eudora 4.0 you select Tools, then Personalities; in Eudora 3.0 you choose Tools, then Options, and click on the Personalities category. One mail

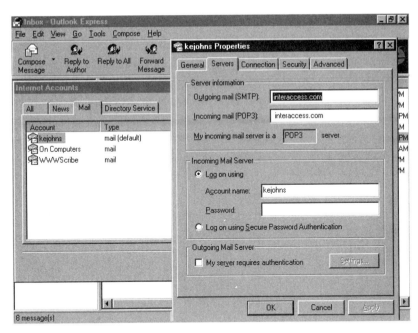

FIGURE 2-16. Microsoft Outlook Express handles multiple e-mail accounts, all of which can be checked with one connection to the Internet. For each account, you specify incoming and outgoing mail servers and other standard configuration information.

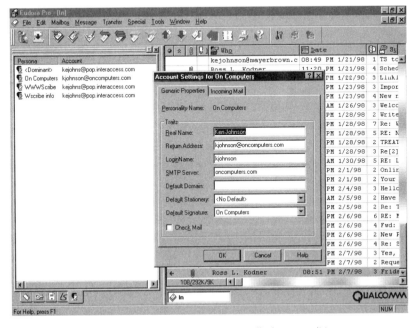

FIGURE 2-17. In Eudora multiple e-mail accounts are called Personalities.

account is the default in both programs (called "dominant" in Eudora) and is always checked. The other accounts can be set up for checking each time. Alternately, you can explicitly tell each program to check the account when connecting to the Internet.

How to Create a Signature

Using a signature is a way of automatically appending additional text to the end of each e-mail message that you send. It saves you from continually having to retype information such as your address. Signature text is kept either within the mail program or in a separate file that you specify in the mail program's options.

Signature text is used for giving additional contact information, such as your firm name, street address, and phone and fax numbers. It can also contain disclaimers saying, for example, that the message does not constitute legal advice or noting that the comments reflect your opinion and not necessarily those of your firm. Some people like to include favorite maxims or other sayings. If you have a Web site, you can include the uniform resource locator (URL) in your signature. Those whose e-mail programs support it can click on the URL, which launches their Web browser and takes them to your Web page. If you use PGP to encrypt your messages, the signature can contain your PGP public key or information on where to obtain it.

At a minimum, the signature text should restate your name and e-mail address. These can be important, particularly if you send e-mail to a mailing list (discussed in Chapter 6). Sometimes your name and e-mail address might not be displayed to the recipients because the mail is shown to be from the mailing list address. Someone who wants to contact you directly can get your address from your signature text. The same is true if one of your messages is forwarded to a third party. With your signature in the message text, that party will know how to contact you.

Netscape Messenger and Outlook Express offer an additional signature option called a vCard card, or Address Book card. This is your personal information, including e-mail address, name, organization, street address, and home and business phone and fax numbers. You can optionally include this Address Book information in each message you send. Recipients using Netscape Messenger or Outlook Express can then put it into their Address Book and create an entry for you. However, since using the vCard card adds quite a few lines of additional text to your messages, you may want to think twice about using it. Most e-mail recipients don't

Signature
Add this signature to all outgoing messages
OK
Cancel
Text
Kenneth E. Johnson, Mayer, Brown and Platt
kejohns@interaccess.com
kejohnson@mayerbrown.com
TECHSHOW 98 Webmaster: http://www.techshow.com
File
Browse...
Don't add signature to Replies and Forwards
Personal Business Card (vCard)
Business cards (vCards) are used to send contact infomation about yourself to others. Select the address book contact to send as your business card.
Card: kejohns@interaccess
Edit...
New...
Attach card to all outgoing messages

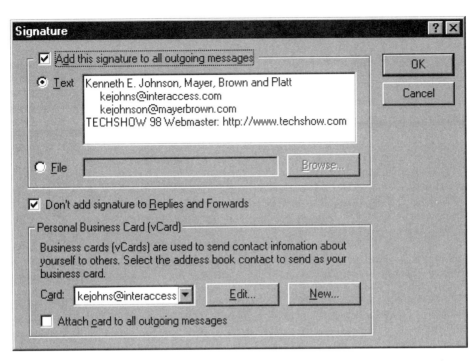

FIGURE 2-18. Outlook Express signature options include using text or the contents of a file, not appending the signature on replies and forwards, and including your vCard entries.

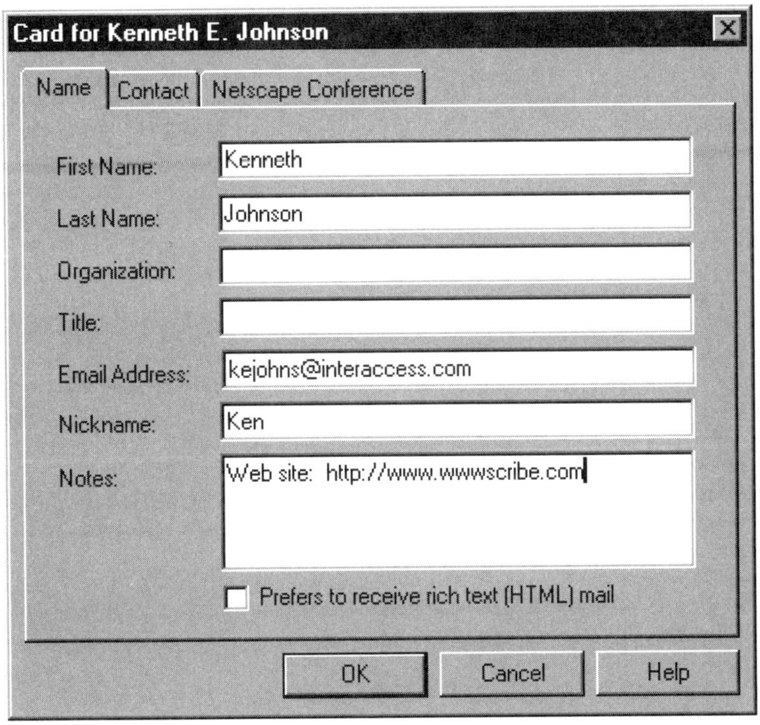

Card for Kenneth E. Johnson
Name
Contact
Netscape Conference
First Name: Kenneth
Last Name: Johnson
Organization:
Title:
Email Address: kejohns@interaccess.com
Nickname: Ken
Notes: Web site: http://www.wwwscribe.com
Prefers to receive rich text (HTML) mail
OK
Cancel
Help

FIGURE 2-19. Netscape Messenger's signature card includes additional contact information about you and can be automatically appended to each message you send.

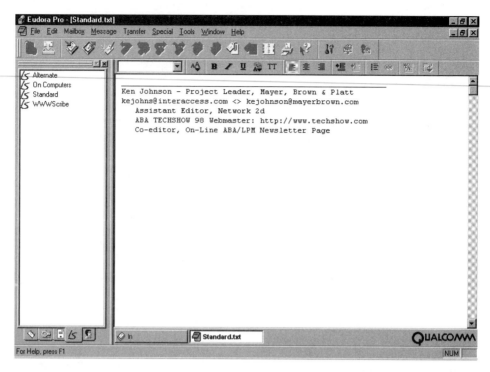

FIGURE 2-20. Eudora Pro allows for multiple signatures, so you can pick which one to use (if any) for each message you create.

like such miscellaneous text because it makes the message larger and thus it takes longer to download from the mail server.

You can have different signature text for different purposes. Eudora Pro supports multiple signatures, beginning with a standard and an alternate signature. The standard signature is the default when new messages are created, but it can be changed. You can also create specific signatures under different Personalities.

You also have the option not to use a signature. When subscribing to a mailing list (as discussed in Chapter 6), you want only the subscription text in the body of the message. Signature text can confuse the mailing list server, which will then send back error messages. In Eudora, you can specify under the message creation toolbar that you do not want to use a signature. In Netscape Messenger and Outlook Express, the signature line is automatically inserted at the end of the message when the New Message window opens. If you don't want a signature, simply delete the text.

FIGURE 2-21. Netscape Messenger inserts the signature text at the bottom of a message when it is prepared.

Finally, two basic rules have emerged on the Internet regarding signatures:

1. **Keep it as short as possible.** Try to keep the number of signature lines to less than four or five. If you need a longer signature for something like a disclaimer or PGP key instructions, don't include a witty quote or promotion for your favorite sports team to make the signature even longer.
2. **Don't use a signature for advertising.** Overt advertising in e-mail messages is frowned upon, particularly when attached (like a signature is) to *every* piece of mail you send, regardless of whether the "advertising" is relevant.

Now that we've configured the program, let's go send some e-mail.

CHAPTER **THREE**

Composing and Sending E-mail

Unless you have a permanent internet connection, all mail you receive goes to your mail server and waits for you to connect to the server and ask for mail. Likewise, messages you create are stored in your Outbox until you connect to the server and send them.

Connecting to the Internet for a Mail Run

The general process of an e-mail run has four basic steps:

1. You connect to your ISP via modem. Your ISP can help you with the programs needed for this connection. (In Windows 95, you use the operating system's Dial-Up Networking program. In Windows 3.x, you have a special type of program called a Winsock, which connects your computer directly to the Internet.)
2. Using the POP and SMTP protocols, you connect to the mail server, receive any waiting messages, and send any messages in your Outbox.
3. Unless you specify otherwise in your e-mail program, mail you've just received is deleted from the mail server so it won't be downloaded again.

4. You disconnect from the Internet and read and write responses to messages "off-line" (i.e., not connected to the Internet). There is no reason you cannot stay connected to the Internet while responding to messages, other than the phone costs.

The actual phone connection time for sending and receiving e-mail is minimal. That's why e-mail is so economical compared to other delivery methods such as faxing, overnight couriers, and the post office.

Before you begin a mail run, you should prepare by doing the following:

- **Check for a local phone number.** If your ISP has multiple dial-up phone numbers, try to find the one closest to your calling location. Ideally, find a number that is within your local calling band so you don't have to pay per-minute charges.
- **Mind a connection break.** If you aren't using a dedicated phone line, make sure other people stay off the phone while you are checking mail. A picked-up extension may cause you to lose your connection.
- **Disable call waiting.** The bane of telecommunications, a call waiting notification can easily break your connection. If you have call

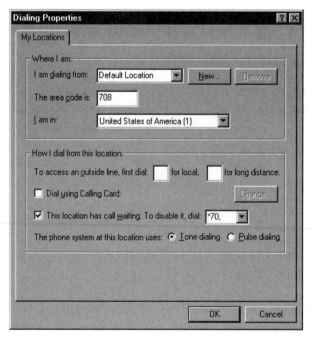

FIGURE 3-1. To avoid a break in the Internet connection when a new phone call comes in, Windows 95 users can disable call waiting through the Modem Dialing Properties dialog box.

waiting, disable it for a particular call by putting *70 in front of the phone number (or whatever code is used to disable call waiting in your area). You can often set your modem to disable call waiting automatically, so you don't have to do it for each call. In Windows 95, this is done by double-clicking on the Modem icon in Control Panel, then selecting the Dialing Properties button. Check the box to disable call waiting, and specify the call waiting code.

◆ **Think about what you're sending.** There is no facility for recalling sent messages once they hit the Internet. If you compose an e-mail message when angry or upset, let the message sit overnight and then read it again. In a calmer light, you'll very likely realize that you don't really want to send the message or that you want to do some major editing before sending it.

Addressing and Address Books

As discussed in the previous chapter, e-mail addresses have a specific format (**user@domain**). While generally these addresses are not case sensitive, traditionally they are given in lowercase.

Every e-mail address has to be absolutely correct, or the message will not go through. Unlike the friendly postal carrier, the Internet cannot get the letter to the right place if you've transposed numbers in the address or misspelled the recipient's name. Correct means three things:

1. The domain name must be correct.
2. The user name must be correct.
3. There must be a valid mail account on that domain under that user name.

Otherwise, the mail will return, or "bounce," back to you with an error message. (Interpreting e-mail error messages is discussed in Appendix A.)

To save you from having to enter the same e-mail address repeatedly (with the possibility of error), e-mail programs include an Address Book feature. Here you can store e-mail addresses, along with the addressees' real names and sometimes additional information such as street address, phone and fax numbers, and related notes.

The full name in the name field displayed in the Address Book doesn't necessarily have to be the one you use. You can specify a shorter name, or nickname, that is easier to remember. When sending mail, you simply select the nickname from the list.

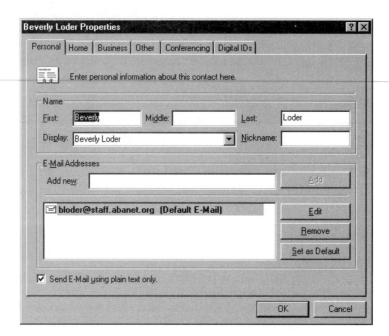

FIGURE 3-2. In addition to e-mail addresses, Microsoft Outlook Express's Address Book includes home and business addresses, notes, Net conferencing information, and digital signatures.

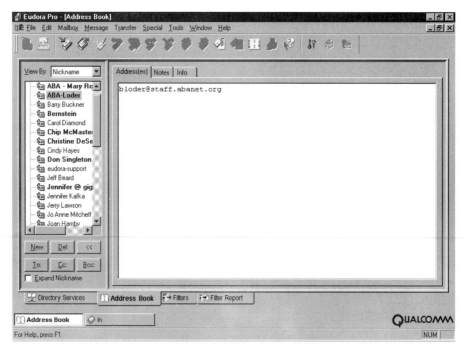

FIGURE 3-3. Here Eudora's Address Book shows entries by nicknames, which are shorthand for e-mail addresses. Entries can also be displayed by e-mail address, full name, and postal address.

It is simple to add new Address Book entries from mail you receive. With the message selected, look for an option called Add to Address Book, or similar wording. The sender's name and e-mail address will go into the Address Book, and you then can add additional information as necessary.

Address book entries are not limited to one individual addressee. You can create group entries under one name, setting up your own distribution lists. When a group entry is selected, your message will simultaneously be sent to everyone on the list. This is a real time saver if you regularly communicate with the same group of people (e.g., on a particular case).

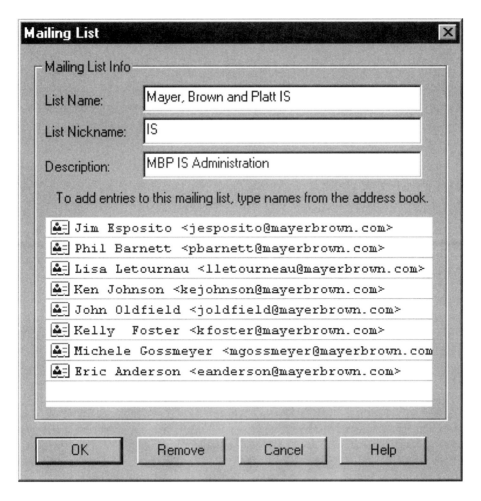

FIGURE 3-4. To create a group entry in Netscape Messenger, first add the individual addressees to the Address Book, then create the mailing list from those names.

Using the To, CC, and BCC Fields

You begin composing an e-mail message by clicking on the New Message or Compose Message button on the toolbar. The New Message window will open with the cursor in the To field. When addressing mail, you have three entries.

The first entry is the To field, for the address of the main recipient of the e-mail message. Multiple addresses can be entered on the To line, separated by spaces, commas, or semicolons. Check your e-mail program for specifics (e.g., Outlook Express uses semicolons and Eudora uses commas). If you pick multiple addresses from the Address Book, they will be inserted in the proper format. As noted, another way to send one message to multiple recipients is to create a group Address Book entry and to specify that entry on the To line.

The second entry, CC, stands for courtesy copy or carbon copy. Addressees inserted here will receive a copy of the message but are not the primary recipients. They will be able to see the addresses in the To field and the other CC addresses. When you receive a message that includes other To and CC addresses, you have the option of replying to only the sender of the message or to the sender and all the other To and CC addresses. The latter is called Reply to All in Eudora and Outlook Express and Reply to Sender and All Recipients in Netscape Messenger.

The next entry, BBC, stands for blind carbon copy. Addressees inserted here will receive a copy of the message but their addresses will not be shown to the To and CC recipients. BCC recipients see the To and CC addresses but not other BCC addresses.

The BCC option is often overlooked, but it can be very useful in enforcing privacy. If you are sending a message to a group of clients, it is inappropriate (and may be a breach of confidentiality) to show all the client names in the To field, since every recipient can see all the other clients' names. Instead, you can address the message to yourself and put each of the client addresses in the BCC field. Thus, each recipient will see only your name and his or her own name on the message.

Apart from the privacy issue, using BCC can be a considerate gesture to your recipients if you are sending the message to many people. Remember, the To and CC recipients see all the other To and CC addresses, and it's frustrating to receive a short message preceded by eight pages of e-mail addresses. For a large distribution, put everyone in the BCC field so the message will be smaller and easier to read.

Using the Subject Line

Always include a subject line, since many people treat messages with
blank subject lines as junk mail and delete the messages without reading
them. Make sure your subject line is relevant to the body of the message,
and make it brief. Long subject lines are truncated in the Inbox display,
which might make the message's real subject unclear.

People receive a lot of e-mail, and you want them to read your message. So, if your message is important, the subject line can contain something like "URGENT!" or "!!!," though unfortunately companies sending
junk mail (also called "spam," as discussed in Appendix A) often use these
types of subjects to get people's attention. It's probably better to be more
specific: "MARY, URGENT" or "BOB, PLEASE READ." Likewise, if the message is just informational, a prefix of "FYI" lets the recipient know that
the message isn't earth-shattering and more-important messages can be
read first.

Typing the Message

After you enter recipients' addresses, and perhaps other sending options,
the cursor moves down to the text area of the window where you type the
actual message. Type as you normally do, and do not to put a hard return
at the end of every line because your e-mail program will automatically
word wrap at the end of each line. If you want to use formatting such as
boldface, indents, or alternate font sizes, and have your e-mail program
set up to do so, use the appropriate buttons on the toolbar. The techniques for typing an e-mail message are relatively the same as those for
any current word processor.

Editing the Message

While you're composing a message, you'll almost certainly want to go
back and edit some of what you've already written. Your e-mail program
uses standard Windows editing features, such as these:

- To reposition anywhere in the message, move the mouse and click
  once to reset the cursor there.
- To reposition the cursor one character at a time, use the arrow keys.

- To move one word to the left, press CTRL+left arrow key; to move one word to the right, press CTRL+right arrow key.
- To move to the beginning of the line, press Home; to move to the end of the line, press End.
- To move to the top of the message, press CTRL+Home; to move to the end of the message, press CTRL+End.
- To select a particular word, double-click on it; to select any amount of text, click and hold the left mouse button, then highlight the desired text.
- To move the selected block of text to a new position on the screen, left-click, hold, and drag the text.

Moving, Copying, and Pasting

Moving, copying, and pasting your message text is easy because, again, each e-mail program uses standard Windows functions and keystrokes. You can also select these from the Edit menu:

- CTRL+X cuts the highlighted text to the Windows clipboard.
- CTRL+C copies the highlighted text to the Windows clipboard.
- CTRL+V copies the text from the Windows clipboard and pastes it into the message at the cursor location.

Don't forget that you can also move, copy, and paste text from a different application. Let's say you have a letter to a client that you want co-counsel to review quickly. Rather than mailing or faxing it, you can copy the text into an e-mail message. You'll probably lose some text formatting, but what's important is the text, not what it looks like. You would follow these steps:

1. Start your e-mail program and your word processor, and open the client letter.
2. Address the e-mail message, and type the preliminary text (e.g., "Lisa, here is the letter I'd like you to review").
3. Press ALT+Tab to go to the letter, and use your mouse to select the text you want to send.
4. Press CTRL+C to copy the text.
5. Press ALT+Tab to return to your e-mail message.
6. Press CTRL+V to paste the text into your message.
7. Send the message.

The entire operation takes less time to complete than it took to type these steps!

Sending with Stationery

Both Eudora Pro and Microsoft Outlook Express allow you to send preformatted or prewritten messages using "stationery." Outlook Express includes a variety of preformatted messages, including Formal Announcement, Birthday, Holiday Letter, and Party Invitation styles. To create a message using stationery, click on the down arrow next to the Compose Message button. From the resulting list of stationery options, pick the desired format or select More Stationary to choose from the Stationery directory.

Eudora Pro's stationery is more properly thought of as template messages. Any message you create can be saved as stationery so it can be used again. This can be very handy if you send the same types of messages repeatedly, such as firm newsletter subscription notices or information on your PGP encryption key. (The encryption program PGP, which stands for Pretty Good Privacy, is discussed in Chapter 8.) Simply create the message, then select Save as Stationery from the File menu. When you want

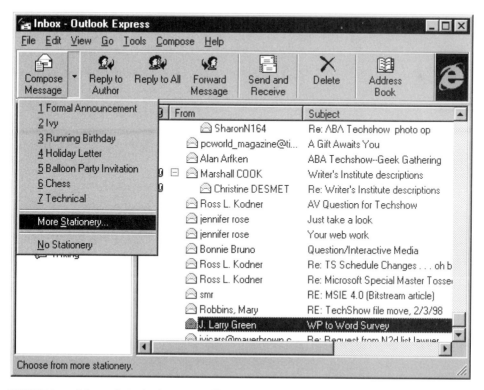

FIGURE 3-5. Microsoft Outlook Express offers a variety of preformatted messages, created from the Compose Message button.

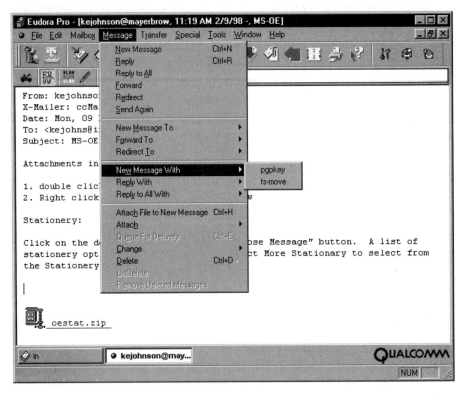

FIGURE 3-6. Once a template message is saved as Eudora Pro stationery, it can be used to send a new message or to reply to a message. Here "pgpkey" and "ts-move" are the stationery names.

to send a message using the stationery, it can be selected from the New Message With, the Reply With, or the Reply to All With options on the Message menu. Edit the message if necessary, then send it.

Understanding Message Formats and E-mail Style Guidelines

The specific format of the messages you send, and the style with which you write them, determines how easily your recipients can read and comprehend your messages. Following a few rules will make you a good e-mail author. Some of these rules, called "Netiquette" (for Internet etiquette) are discussed later, but a few points are in order first.

Formatting Availability

Traditionally e-mail messages have been straight ASCII text, meaning that they consist of only the standard keyboard characters (along with a few

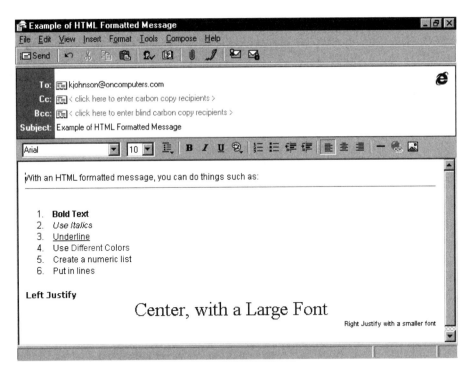

FIGURE 3-7. HTML formatting, used here in Microsoft Outlook Express, provides formatting options beyond straight text. Some older e-mail programs, however, do not support HTML.

symbols). Hence, there's not much fancy formatting available, although asterisks and underscores have evolved as formatting tags for text messages. They are used on both sides of a word or phrase to represent *bold* and _italics , respectively.

Now, however, a new format—HyperText Markup Language—is being supported in e-mail programs. HTML is the "coding" used to create Web pages. By using the same codes in an e-mail message, you can format using various fonts and font sizes, boldface, italics, underlines, text colors, center and right alignment, and bullets.

Unfortunately, some e-mail programs, particularly the older ones, do not support HTML formatting. The message format that recipients actually see depends on their own mail program. Some may see only the plain text, or plain text with an HTML attachment (which they can view in their Web browser to see the formatting). Some recipients may see the message full of HTML tags, making it difficult to read. Use HTML formatting only when sending to people whom you know have an e-mail program that supports it. Both Netscape Messenger and Outlook Express let you indicate in the Address Book whether the addressee can receive HTML-formatted messages.

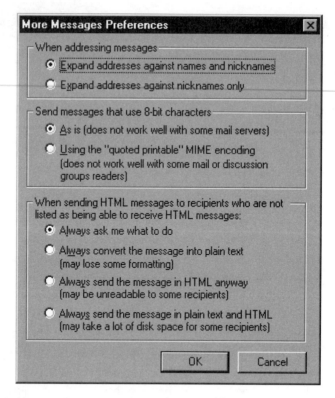

FIGURE 3-8. In Netscape Messenger, you can be warned before sending HTML-formatted messages if the Address Book shows that the intended recipient cannot receive such messages.

Eudora Pro 4.0 has an additional option for viewing HTML-formatted messages: using Microsoft Internet Explorer as a viewer for such messages. If Microsoft Internet Explorer 4.0 is not already on your computer, the Eudora install program will optionally install it. Eudora Pro's built-in viewer will handle most of the basic HTML formatting, such as font attributes, bulleted lists, text justification, hyperlinks, horizontal lines, and some embedded graphics. Using Internet Explorer as the HTML viewer, however, adds the ability to view embedded GIF, PNG, and JPEG images, along with numbered lists, tables and forms, international character sets, Java applets, JavaScript, ActiveX controls, and dynamic HTML. To activate the Internet Explorer viewer (if not specified when you install Eudora Pro 4.0), select Tools, Options, and Viewing Mail, then check Use Microsoft's Viewer.

Message Composition

When it comes to e-mail composition, there are some generally agreed-upon style points for creating good messages.

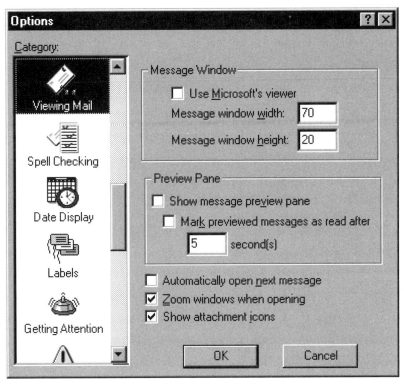

FIGURE 3-9. To use Microsoft Internet Explorer as Eudora Pro 4.0's HTML viewer, make the setting under the Viewing Mail Options.

◆ **Use short paragraphs.** Most e-mail messages are read on a computer screen. Long paragraphs mean the reader has to use the scroll bars, and it's easy to lose one's place, so paragraphs should fit easily on one screen.

◆ **Be concise, but don't kill the understanding.** People like receiving short e-mail messages that are to the point. Long, rambling messages are harder to read and to understand, and they take longer to download from the mail server. Don't, however, make your messages so short that it's impossible to understand what you're trying to say. This is especially true with replies.

◆ **Run the spelling checker.** Most current e-mail programs include an integrated spelling checker. Use it. Although much e-mail is informal, there is no reason to send messages with spelling errors. If your mail program doesn't include a spelling checker, create the message in your word processor, spell check it there, then copy and paste the text into the e-mail message. (You may want to grammar check while you're at it.)

◆ **Reread the message before sending it.** Review your message to check for sense and typos, and also to ensure that you really want to send it. If you're angry or upset, or there's any question about whether or not to send the message, sleep on it. Remember that you can't recall a message once it hits the Internet.

◆ **Don't overuse abbreviations, smileys, and emoticons.** Abbreviations, while they're often silly, are sometimes handy in informal messages. They are generally inappropriate for business correspondence, however, since some recipients won't know what they mean. Smileys are punctuation symbols arranged to show emotion. Again, they might not be appropriate for business correspondence. Emoticons are similar to smileys in that they convey the author's tone. (Some of the more common of these shortcuts are shown in Table 3-1.)

Abbreviations, smileys, and emoticons provide a way to shorten messages, to show emotion, and to give inflection and tone to written messages. While we clue in on these things in spoken conversation, they are very hard to convey in written form. As useful as they are, however, these shortcuts can potentially lead to trouble if someone quotes your e-mail message (verbally or in another medium) and leaves out the smiley or emoticon. It can completely change the tone of what you've said, particularly when the smiley or emoticon shows that you were joking about

TABLE 3-1. COMMON E-MAIL ABBREVIATIONS, SMILEYS, AND EMOTICONS

Abbreviations		Smileys (Turn your head sideways to the left to read them)		Emoticons
BTW	By the Way	:-)	Smiling	<grin>
FYI	For Your Information	;-)	Winking	<g> (also signi-
IMHO	In My Humble Opinion (rarely humble)	:-<	Frowning	fying a grin
		:-@	Screaming	<smile>
LOL	Laughing Out Loud			<sigh>
ROTFL	Rolling on the Floor, Laughing			
TIA	Thanks in Advance			
TTFN	Ta Ta for Now			

what you just said. Consider this in an e-mail message: "I worked until midnight on this case. Man, if it wasn't for what I'm charging him, I'd hate this client! ;-)." The "wink" indicates that you're just kidding about hating the client, but what if, perhaps in a letter to the client, someone quotes these sentences without the smiley? It thoroughly alters your meaning, even though the words are exactly as you wrote them.

Following E-mail Netiquette

Since there is no formal standard for e-mail communications, what you say in a message can easily be misinterpreted. The text format of e-mail makes it hard to convey nuance, inflection, and other expressive signals we normally discern in verbal communications. In addition, because of the speed of e-mail, an e-mail "conversation" tends to be more informal than other written communications. This speed often discourages thoughtful replies. You may not see this informality as a problem, yet your clients may expect an e-mail message to convey the same level of formality as a business letter.

To help e-mail writers, Internet users have developed, somewhat by consensus, basic guidelines for what to do—and what not to do—when sending e-mail. These guidelines are known as Netiquette. There is Netiquette for just about every part of the Internet—for e-mail, newsgroups, Web pages, mailing lists (discussed in Chapter 6), and so forth. Here are some e-mail Netiquette points:

- **Again, think before you send.** Remember that messages can't be retrieved once they've been sent, and messages are typically kept by the recipient**s.** Anything you write can be referred back to you, sometimes much later. If there is a question about the message, wait a while and see if you still really want to send it.
- **If you wouldn't want something to be public knowledge, don't put it in e-mail.** Your e-mail theoretically can be read by the systems administrator in charge of your home mail server, by administrators at each network through which the message passes, and by the administrator at the recipient's home mail server. A common Internet saying is not to put anything in a message that you wouldn't want to see posted by the office water cooler. Even if you encrypt the message so only the recipient can read it, that person can decode it and forward it on to others as plain text.
- **If security is important, encrypt your messages.** PGP is a good encryption choice and is currently available as an integrated add-

on for Eudora, with additional mail program support anticipated for the near future. (PGP message encryption is reviewed in Chapter 8.)

- **Don't use ALL CAPS.** Using all capital letters LOOKS LIKE YOU ARE SHOUTING! Use mixed case instead, and use all caps only when necessary.

- **Watch your tone.** Because you're not in a face-to-face conversation, it's easy for tempers to get out of hand. Be careful how you phrase things.

- **Remember that sarcasm and humor don't travel well.** Because of the text format, sarcasm might be overlooked or interpreted literally, so that the reader perceives a meaning opposite of your intended one. Jokes and humor could be read as criticism. (This is one reason for the <g> and <grin> emoticons, to show that you're being humorous.)

- **Be concise, especially when replying with quoted text.** It's easy for the mind to wander when reading long messages on a computer screen. It's frustrating to have to scroll through mounds of quoted text just to get to a reply. Quote only enough of the original message to give the proper context for your response.

- **Make subject lines relevant.** If you're exchanging replies with someone and the topic of the conversation changes, change the subject line to reflect the new topic. You can append "was…" at the end of the subject to show the change. For example, if you started talking about document assembly and are now discussing Wisconsin microbrews, the subject line might say something like "Re: Wisconsin Beers (was Document Assembly)."

- **Be patient with recipients.** Six hours after sending the first message, don't fire off a follow-up message with "Why didn't you answer my e-mail?" Remember that few people check their e-mail hourly. It may be off-work hours (particularly overseas) or a holiday you don't know about, or the recipient may be sick or on vacation. The message may be delayed because of problems on the Internet or on that particular mail server.

- **Ask for clarification.** If you're unclear about what someone means in his or her message, ask the person nicely for a clarification. Don't assume.

- **Understand the importance of international Netiquette.** If you reference dates and times in a message, be specific. For example, is "I'll call you at 10 a.m." referring to your time zone or the recipient's time zone? You may want to use Greenwich Mean Time as your point of reference ("I'll call you at 6 a.m. GMT"), so it can easily be translated to local time wherever the recipient is located. Likewise, be specific about types of monetary units. In your contact information, include the proper international dialing codes. Be *very* careful with humor. Different countries and cultures have very different perceptions of what is funny and what is appropriate.

◆ **Don't pass along chain letters and hoaxes.** Don't use e-mail to send chain letters or blindly pass along requests for help and virus warnings, most of which are hoaxes.

◆ **Reconsider passing along that joke.** While a joke may be funny, getting lots of jokes (many of which are duplicates) can be very annoying when you're in a rush. A friend of mine was out of the office for a few days, and when she returned almost two-thirds of her e-mail messages were jokes. Dealing with those while trying to find the important things in her Inbox took much of the humor out of the material received.

What Are Those Flames in Your E-mail?

An additional Netiquette edict that requires special emphasis is the need to avoid "flaming." A flame refers to a verbal attack in e-mail form, a critical and disparaging message intended to provoke the recipient's anger. These generally arise in mailing lists and newsgroup postings. If you get flamed and respond in kind, this starts a "flame war." Angry and insulting messages fly back and forth, the participants forget what started the whole thing but continue with the attacks, and eventually one person wears out and doesn't respond anymore. The best way to win a flame war is to not partake in the first place.

There are several ways to get yourself flamed:

◆ SEND MESSAGES IN ALL CAPS. You're shouting again.

◆ Criticize someone's spelling, grammar, or punctuation.

◆ Send messages that are blatant advertising or include advertising copy in your signature line.

◆ Request help with something but don't give enough information for someone to help you. A message like "My WordPerfect doesn't work" fails to state a specific problem, and it also fails to indicate the version of WordPerfect (e.g., 5.1 or 8.0, for Windows 95 or the Macintosh) to which you're referring.

◆ Ask for information that is readily available elsewhere. A great example of this is to send a message to a mailing list asking how to unsubscribe. This information is sent to you when you first subscribe and is also available from the mailing list software through a help request.

So what if you need to vent to someone in a message? One standard is to use two special emoticons: <Flame on> and <Flame off>. The text between these is generally understood to signify frustrations coming out, and it does not need any reply. (Remember, you're not trying to start a flame war.)

Requesting Return Receipts

Some e-mail programs, such as Eudora and Netscape Messenger, let you request a Return Receipt for messages you send. While return receipts work well on internal mail systems all running on the same mail server, the same cannot be said when sending Internet e-mail across multiple servers and different mail programs. Even if you specify a return receipt, you probably will not get any notification when the message is read.

If it is important to know whether a message is received, the easiest thing to do is to put a note in the message text asking the recipient to reply immediately to confirm the message's receipt. Alternatively, just pick up the phone and call the recipient.

Now that you know how to compose and send e-mail, it's time to move on to receiving and replying to messages.

*CHAPTER***FOUR**

Receiving and Replying to E-mail

YOUR E-MAIL ARRIVES ON YOUR MAIL SERVER, waiting for you to transfer, or download, the messages. You can then review and respond to them as necessary.

Checking for Incoming E-mail

When you're ready to get your e-mail, you choose the Check Mail, Get Mail, or Send and Receive button to make the connection and retrieve your mail (or you may configure your mail program to check for mail automatically when the program's opened). New messages go into your Inbox, typically below the already read messages, with an icon or some formatting indicating that they're new. You double-click on the Inbox item to read the message. Then you can keep, reply to, forward, redirect, store, print, or delete the message.

If you'll be connected to the Internet for any length of time (perhaps you do some mammoth Web surfing on weekends), you can set your e-mail program to check for new messages at certain intervals. This can

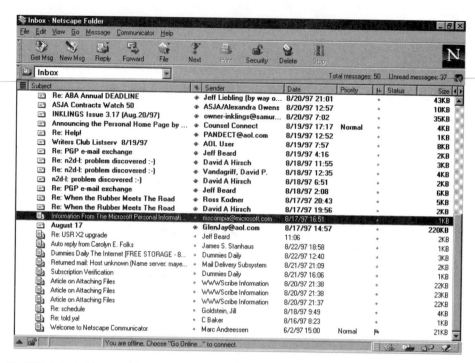

FIGURE 4-1. In Netscape Messenger's Inbox, new messages are displayed in bold with an envelope icon. Read messages show the "letter" out of the envelope.

also be done if you have a full-time, or nearly full-time, Internet connection. The benefit is that you needn't remember to check for mail; it happens automatically. Eudora and Outlook Express can play a sound to notify you whenever new mail arrives, which is especially convenient with a full-time connection, when you're often doing something else on the computer.

If you aren't connected regularly, you should unselect the Check Mail option, or set the automatic check time interval to zero, which disables it. The reason for this is that you only want to connect when you say so. Having your computer dial up the Internet when you're on the phone, or you're finishing a brief that's due in ten minutes, is inconvenient and frustrating.

Reading the Message Header

Every message you receive includes a message header, which carries information about the message's delivery. It contains the basic To, From, and

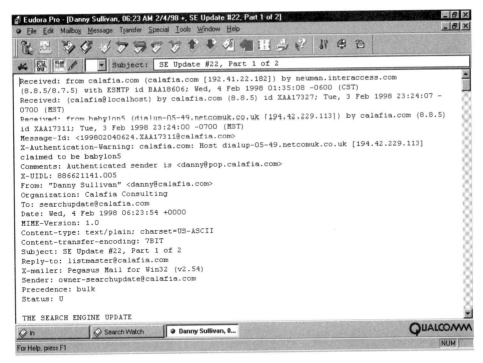

FIGURE 4-2. To see the entire message header in Eudora Pro, click on the "Blah" button on the toolbar.

Subject information, and additional information gets added along the way. Thankfully, you'll often see only a part of the header, though you can choose to view all the manifold details if so moved.

Reviewing the header can provide some interesting information about how the message came to you. It is also useful for setting filters to manage your e-mail (as discussed in Chapter 5) and evaluating where junk messages came from (as discussed in Appendix A). The following are some of the header fields:

- **Subject, To, CC, and From:** These provide the standard information displayed in every message.
- **Received:** These lines are put in by each mail server as the message makes its way to you. Reading from bottom to top, you'll see the route the message took.
- **Date:** This shows the date and time the message was sent.
- **Reply-to:** This indicates the address where replies should be directed, if not to the From address.
- **Message-ID:** This is a machine-generated identifier for this message.

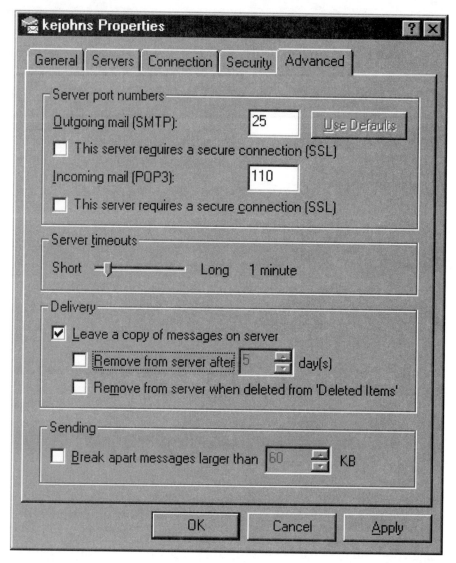

FIGURE 4-3. Microsoft Outlook Express lets you keep e-mail on the mail server and optionally delete it after a certain number of days. Another option is to delete it from the server when the message is deleted from the program's Trash folder. Eudora provides this same capability.

- ◆ **Status:** This is added by *your* e-mail program and indicates whether the message was unread or previously read.
- ◆ **X-items:** These are nonstandard headers added by mail programs for their own use. For example, X-UIDL is used by Eudora to determine which messages were already downloaded, X-Mailer indicates the name of the program used to create the message, and X-Info specifies information about the mail server.

Should Messages Be Copied or Moved?

One question discussed briefly in Chapter 2 is whether to copy or move e-mail off the mail server when you download it. You have the option of leaving messages on the mail server, which means they'll be downloaded again the next time you check for e-mail (though they'll appear in your Inbox marked as having been read). In Eudora and Microsoft Outlook Express you can leave mail on the server but automatically delete it after a specified number of days.

Why would you want to leave messages on the server after you download them? Most commonly the reason is that you use more than one computer (and perhaps more than one e-mail program) to check your mail, but one computer or program is your primary one and you want to manage all your messages there. If you check your e-mail from another computer, you still want those messages to be downloaded by your primary computer so you can keep everything together. The way to do this is by configuring the other mail program to leave mail on the server while setting your primary mail program to delete the messages once downloaded.

Let's look at an example. Say you use Eudora Pro on your computer at the firm but are going to be traveling with a laptop that has Microsoft Internet Explorer and Outlook Express. You want to check your e-mail while on the road, but you want to be able to download any important messages through Eudora when you're back in the office. You can accomplish this by following these steps:

1. You probably already have Eudora configured to delete e-mail after downloading it. Keep those settings.
2. Configure Outlook Express (under the configuration's Advanced options) to leave the messages on the server. Check the box that says "Remove from server when deleted from 'Deleted Items.'" Under the General options, check the box that says "Empty messages from the 'Deleted Items' folder on exit."
3. Then, when traveling, check your e-mail using Outlook Express. You can leave any important messages in the Inbox or move them to a folder. Any messages that you do *not* want to keep in Eudora should be deleted. The next time you connect to get your e-mail, Outlook Express will delete these from the mail server and you won't see them again.
4. When you are back in the office, collect your mail with Eudora. The messages you didn't delete with Outlook Express will be

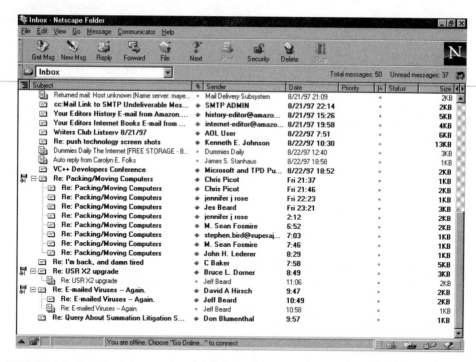

FIGURE 4-4. Netscape Messenger can optionally display message threads as nested messages in the Inbox. This shows how the messages are related and also allows you to read them in order.

downloaded, just as if they were new messages, then (finally) deleted from the server.

Replying to E-mail

It's time to reply to some of those messages in your Inbox. Usually you want to reply to a message instead of starting an entirely new message as a response. By replying, you keep the same subject (typically with a Re: prefix, showing a reply). This creates a thread—a series of responses to the original message. By reading the thread, as indicated by the Re: subject lines, following the chain of information exchanged is easy. This can be particularly important if more than two people are responding to the message. Both Netscape Messenger and Outlook Express can display threaded messages together, making it easier to read the messages in threaded order.

Before you reply, check the other messages in your Inbox to see if there are any additional messages from that author. It may be that someone with a request has sent you a subsequent message saying "Never mind." It's better to find that out initially rather than waste time crafting a reply that is unnecessary.

In addition, be sure that replying is appropriate. If you received a CC on the message, answering may not be necessary (or desirable).

Lastly, if you receive a message that will require extra time to reply to in full, it is a nice gesture to send a brief reply letting the sender know that you received the message and you will send a longer reply later.

Replying to Sender or to All

When replying to a message that includes other To and CC addresses, you need to decide whether to include those others in your response. Eudora, Netscape Messenger, and Outlook Express all let you reply either to the sender only or to all addressees on the original message. This latter option is called Reply to All. The original sender's address is put in the To field, and everyone else's address is put in the CC field.

If your response is appropriate for the whole group, use Reply to All. Even then, you can still remove individual addresses from the CC field if needed. If your message is meant only for the sender, reply only to that

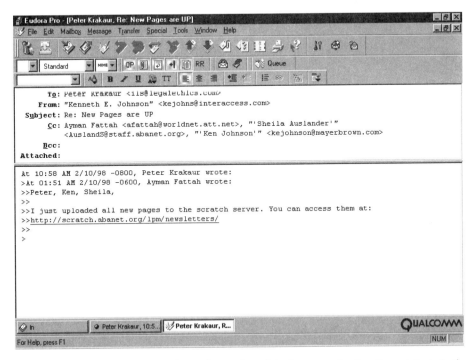

FIGURE 4-5. This Eudora Pro Reply to All puts the original message's other To recipients in the CC field of the reply.

party. Watch out for message threads, since some of these turn into two-way conversations, in which you don't need to keep including other people.

Some older e-mail programs, such as version 2 of Eudora, don't have the Reply to All feature. If, however, you do want to reply to every addressee on the original message, you can copy the addresses out of the original and paste them into your reply's CC field.

Quoting Dos and Don'ts

E-mail programs can automatically include the original message text in your reply. This is called quoting, and it provides a context for your response—that is, recipients know to what you are responding. Quoted text generally appears with a greater than sign (>) in front of each line, though you can sometimes change this character or include additional formatting such as italics. Automatic quoting can be turned off, but it is best not to do so. If you have quoting turned on and decide you don't want to in-

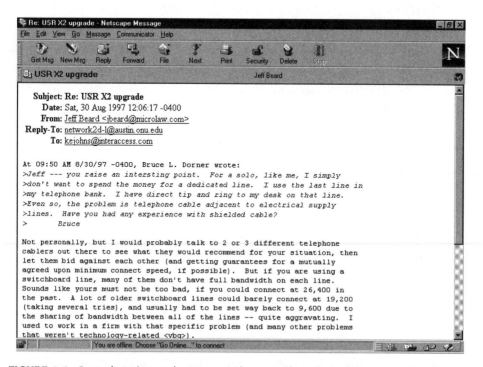

FIGURE 4-6. Quoted text in a reply appears with greater than signs at the start of each line. Netscape Messenger can optionally display the text in colored italics as well.

clude anything from the original message, you can quickly highlight the quoted text with your mouse and hit the Delete key.

One useful feature of quoting is the ability to intermix your reply with the quoted text, enabling you to respond to each item in the original message at the proper point.

Quoting can easily get out of hand, so e-mail authors follow a few rules:

- **You don't have to quote the entire message.** Cut the quoted text to just enough to provide a context for your answers. Message threads can become a nightmare if everyone always quotes the entire message. You'll have to go through pages of quotes just to learn what the response is. Moreover, each time a message is quoted, another greater than sign is put at the beginning of the line. As the number of replies increases, the number of ">>>" expands quickly. This makes the message increasingly harder to read, especially since the greater than signs can cause the lines to wrap in strange places. Always take out previously quoted text that's no longer necessary.
- **You do want to quote enough.** Don't completely cut out quoting just to make small and concise replies. No one likes getting a reply that says something like, "Yes." Yes to what? Include enough to make sense of what you are saying.
- **<snip> quoted text.** If you delete in the middle of a quoted block, include <snip> or [. . . .] to show that some original text was removed.
- **Don't edit quoted text.** Don't change quoted text written by someone else. Doing so is tantamount to forgery.

Forwarding Messages

Rather than replying to a message, sometimes you may want to forward it on to someone else. Forwarding is similar to replying, except that you have to fill in the To address. The subject line typically has a Fwd: prefix, indicating to the recipient that this is a forwarded message. The original text of the message is quoted.

It's easy to go overboard with forwarding. Much of the Internet's bandwidth is taken up with jokes (half of them are about Microsoft or Bill Gates), with false charity letters (a sick boy is collecting cards), and with virus hoaxes (opening a message with the subject "Good Times" will wipe out your hard drive—which is debunked in Appendix A). Before you for-

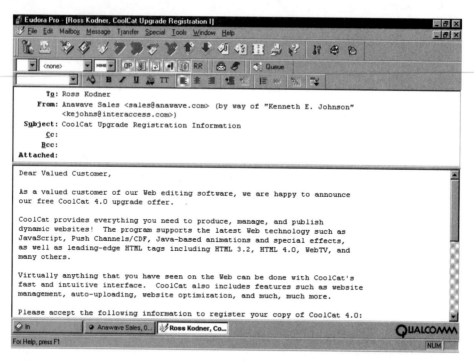

FIGURE 4-7. A redirected message in Eudora Pro shows that it is "by way of" your e-mail account.

ward a message, consider whether it's really necessary for that person to get that message.

Eudora offers another forward option called Redirect, in which a message is sent to a new recipient "by way of" you. It can be used, for example, if a message is sent to you by mistake and you know the intended recipient. When the message is redirected, the original sender's address appears in the From field, along with "by way of" your address. The message text appears in normal style and is not quoted.

CHAPTER **FIVE**

Managing Your E-mail

IT'S EASY TO BECOME OVERWHELMED WITH E-MAIL, particularly from mailing lists (which can generate dozens of messages a day, as discussed in Chapter 6). To keep a handle on your e-mail, you need to manage it—delete messages that aren't necessary, store messages that you want to keep, and filter messages as they come into your Inbox.

Filtering Messages

Filters are rules on how to handle incoming messages. Typically filtering is used to direct messages to certain folders or mailboxes automatically. It helps you to organize by putting messages into their proper places, and it keeps you from missing important messages amid the unimportant ones in your Inbox. Filtering can also help with unsolicited, junk e-mail (a.k.a. "spam," considered in Appendix A) by automatically moving it to someplace other than the Inbox.

Most current e-mail programs allow you to do basic filtering, though some offer more-advanced options, such as filtering on different message header items. Among the standard mail programs, Eudora Light offers basic filtering, while Eudora Pro has very robust filtering with many

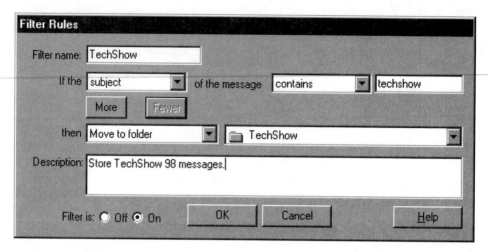

FIGURE 5-1. In Netscape Messenger this filter will direct all messages with a subject containing "techshow" to the TechShow folder.

options. Although Netscape Navigator, in versions 2 and 3, has no mail filtering, Netscape Messenger offers standard filtering.

Microsoft Outlook Express's filtering, called the Inbox Assistant, also offers standard filtering. Microsoft Internet Mail offers only very basic filtering. (Table 5-1 summarizes the filtering capabilities of the three e-mail programs discussed herein.)

Eudora Pro offers the most filtering options, including filtering on outgoing mail and filters that can be run manually. Many conditions can be tested, including text in a variety of fields in the message header. Matching can be on contains, doesn't contain, is, is not, begins with, ends with, appears, and doesn't appear. Two conditions can be checked (joined by and, or, unless), and up to five actions can be performed.

Eudora and Outlook Express offer a filtering option to delete mail from the server without downloading it. Such filtered mail will "disappear" without you seeing it. This is an excellent feature if you're getting junk e-mail from a particular address. By setting up this type of filter, you will never see that junk mailer's future messages, and you will not have to spend the time downloading them. Just be careful that you don't define the filter so it can work against legitimate messages.

To see filtering at work, let's look at a fairly complex example in Eudora Pro. We want to know when a message comes in from a particular person (Barry Brickner) and includes a CC to another specific person (Ross Kodner). When those conditions are met, Eudora will play a sound,

TABLE 5-1. E-MAIL PROGRAM FILTERING CAPABILITIES

	Eudora Pro	Netscape Messenger	Outlook Express
Filter timing	Incoming or outgoing messages, or run manually	Incoming messages only	Incoming messages only
Filter on any item in the message header	Yes	No	No
Filter on the body text	Yes	Yes	No
Filter: text is, isn't, begins with, ends with, doesn't contain	Yes	Yes	No
Filter: appears, doesn't appear	Yes	No	No
Filter on e-mail account	Yes (in Eudora Pro 4.0)	No	Yes
Filter on message size	No	No	Yes
Action: change priority	Yes	Yes	No
Action: change status	Mark as read, unread, replied, forwarded, or redirected	Mark as read, watch thread, or ignore thread	No
Action: forward	Yes	No	Yes
Action: redirect	Yes	No	No
Action: reply with template message	Yes	No	Yes
Action: notify user	Yes	No	No
Action: delete from server	Yes	No	Yes
Action: do not download from server	No	No	Yes
Toggle individual filters on and off	No	Yes	Yes
Filter report	Yes	No	No

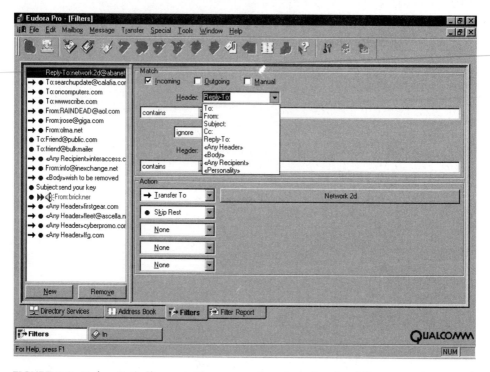

FIGURE 5-2. Eudora Pro's filters provide many options, including the ability to examine several message heading fields.

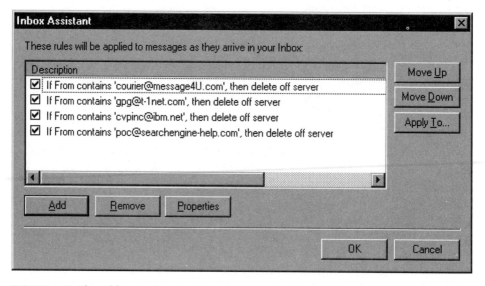

FIGURE 5-3. The addresses described here represent junk e-mail I've received. The Microsoft Outlook Express filters will delete these messages from the mail server without downloading them to my Inbox.

change the priority and label of the message, and copy it to a folder (by copying it, it remains in the Inbox). Set up the filter like this:

1. Match on Incoming Mail.
2. For the first condition, match on Header From: Contains Brickner. You're using a name and not the specific e-mail address for a reason—Brickner may change his e-mail address, but if his mail is configured for his "real name" (see Chapter 2), the From: will always come with "Brickner" in it.
3. Here you want two conditions to be met, so specify "**and**" between them.
4. For the second condition, match on Header CC: Contains Kodner.
5. Under the first Action, select **Play Sound.** Using the [...] button, select the sound file to play.
6. For the second Action, select **Make Priority**, and select the desired priority from the drop-down list. (Eudora offers Highest, High, Normal, Low, and Lowest priorities.)

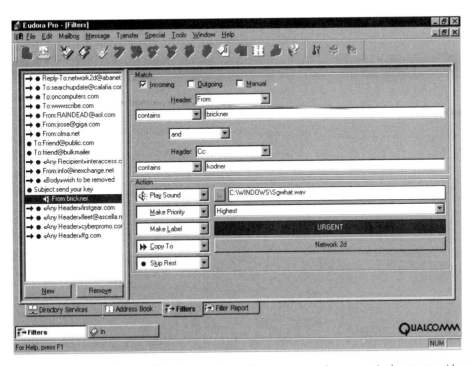

FIGURE 5-4. This Eudora Pro filter is set up based on a message from a particular name, with a CC to another name. When those conditions are met, a sound is played, the message's priority and label are changed, and the message is copied to a specific folder.

7. For the third Action, select Make Label, then select the appropriate label. (Eudora has seven labels, which you can customize by color and name.)

8. For the fourth Action, select **Copy To** and specify the name of the mailbox where you want Eudora to copy the message.

9. The final Action is **Skip Rest.** This simply tells Eudora that filtering on this message is done. No other filters should be run on this message, and the filters start again with the next message.

Filters are further explored in Appendix A, which discusses how to set up filters to take care of junk e-mail.

Storing Messages

You should keep the messages in your Inbox (and Outbox) to a minimum by putting messages that you want to keep in specific mailboxes or folders. These folders have the same format as the Inbox, and you can reply, forward, and redirect messages from folders just like you do from the Inbox. You can create folders based on the sender or topic. (Clients and matters make good folder subjects.) When you first start using e-mail, your folders will be fairly general—but they will quickly become more specific as you get more messages.

Don't forget about storing the e-mail that you've sent. This provides a record of what you've written and is often as important as the messages you've received. Eudora's outgoing filters are a good way to do this automatically.

Folders are not the only places to store e-mail. Most mail programs let you save messages as text files, which can then be imported into word processing documents, a database, your contact manager, and the like. You can also copy and paste all or part of a message into another program by using the Windows CTRL+C and CTRL+V keys, respectively.

One of my favorite tools is askSam, a free-form database popular in law offices. It includes an import filter that can read a Eudora mailbox and create a database of its messages. You first need to store all the appropriate messages in one or more mailboxes. Then, in askSam, either create a new database or open an existing one. Select File and Import from the menu. In the Import window, choose Eudora (*.MBX) as the File Type, set the Directory to the Eudora directory, and select the correct mailbox or mailboxes under File Name.

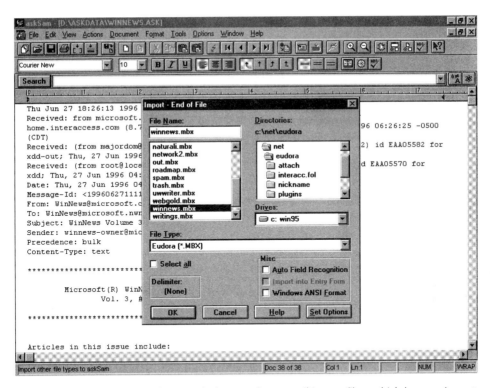

FIGURE 5-5. The program askSam includes a Eudora e-mail import filter, which lets you import an entire Eudora mailbox of messages into the database.

Deleting Messages

Do not fill your hard drive and folders with useless messages. Get in the habit of processing messages in your Inbox right away. Occasionally go through the remaining items in the Inbox, along with the Outbox/Sent Items and other folders, and delete those items that you no longer need. With threaded messages that include quoted text, you can often delete all but the most recent message, since that message will include the text from previous messages.

Deleted messages are put into the Trash (or Deleted Items) folder, so they can be "undeleted" if necessary. You can either delete items from the Trash manually or specify that you want to empty the Trash whenever you exit the mail program. Remember, though, that when a message is deleted from the Trash, it's gone for good.

Checking E-mail from Another Computer

At times you might be away from your computer (and e-mail program) and need to check your e-mail. You have three options.

Use Someone Else's Web Browser

If you have access to an Internet connection and a Web browser—such as Netscape Navigator, Netscape Communicator, or Internet Explorer—you can temporarily configure its mail program to access your e-mail. Enter your e-mail information, including the POP and SMTP servers, as discussed in Chapter 2. For security's sake, don't put your password in the configuration; type it in when prompted. When you're done receiving your mail, delete all the messages (or forward them on and delete them from the Outbox), delete them from the Trash, and remove your information from the mail program's configuration settings. Remember, however, that both Eudora and Outlook Express have an option to delete mail from the server when it is deleted from the Trash. If you want to keep the messages on the server, make sure this option is not set.

Retrieving e-mail through someone else's Web browser, though not difficult, does have security problems. Though you might delete the messages, they may still be readable in the browser program's cache (the information is often not deleted until the space is needed for something else). At a minimum, manually clear the cache before exiting the program, which is done through the Options settings. Even then, the data can possibly be recovered directly from the hard drive by someone who knows where (and how) to look for it.

Grab Your Mail from the Web

Several Web-based services allow you to check your own e-mail account from their Web sites. You only need a Web browser, and no configuration changes are required. Two such sites are EmuMail (http://www.emumail.net/) and MailStart.Com (http://www.mailstart.com/).

Again, there may be security concerns—the Web pages with your messages may be stored in the browser's cache. Manually clear the cache before exiting the program.

Use Web-Based Mail

Chapter 1 mentions Yahoo Mail (http://mail.yahoo.com), a Web-based mail system that allows you to retrieve your e-mail with only a Web browser.

FIGURE 5-6. EmuMail.net lets you check your mail from its Web site, using any Web browser.

With a service such as RocketMail, you can get your mail from any Internet connection and Web browser—though the "empty the cache" admonition still applies.

CHAPTER **SIX**

Using Mailing Lists for Global Discussions

L AWYERS HAVE DISCOVERED MAILING LISTS with a vengeance in the past few years. These lists are a place to stay in touch with colleagues, to have questions answered, and to keep up on legal (and nonlegal) developments. It all happens right from your Inbox.

Why Mailing Lists?

Mailing lists are e-mail discussion groups, where messages are automatically distributed to all members of the group. The mailing list has a single e-mail address, but messages sent to that address are resent to all the people who have joined the list.

You begin by subscribing to the list through an e-mail request to the program that handles the mailing list messages. When you subsequently send a message to the mailing list address, everyone who has also subscribed gets a copy of the message. When someone replies to a message, each subscriber gets a copy of the reply. In essence, everyone sees everyone's messages. You'll see a variety of topics—and a variety of different opinions on those topics. As you can imagine, lists can generate many messages each day.

The technical side of mailing lists—forwarding each individual message to many addresses—is automated by a mailing list program. These programs are often generically called "listservs" or "listservers." LISTSERV, however, refers to a specific, commercial mailing list software. Another popular program is Majordomo, a free mailing list manager that runs on UNIX computers. You really don't need to worry about the type of program that runs the list. Although there are some differences in how you subscribe to lists and obtain help in the different programs, the programs basically function the same way. The person or organization that makes the list available and handles the administrative duties related to the hardware and software (e.g., fixing errors when they occur) is referred to as the list owner.

From a subscriber's perspective, there are three different types of mailing lists:

- **Announcement Only.** The list is used to distribute mail from the list owner only. No replies can be sent to the list, so no replies are redistributed. Announcement lists are popular with vendors and organizations who need to get information to their members. Law firms also can use these lists to distribute newsletters and other material to clients.
- **Moderated.** The list owner monitors the messages before redistribution. Off-topic, inappropriate, or Netiquette-violating messages are not distributed to the list subscribers, so the list is very focused on its reason for being. Moderators are either editors or censors, depending on who you ask (and when you ask them).
- **Unmoderated.** The list has no human intervention in the distribution of messages. The list owner generally stays in the background unless a problem with the list occurs. The discussions are wide-ranging and frequently go off topic (which isn't necessarily a bad thing). I've seen a legal technology list take a few side trips into British sport cars, the best restaurants in New York, the battle of the microbrews, ultralight aircraft, "you might be a hillbilly lawyer if . . .," and the joys of the Pacific Coast Highway in California.

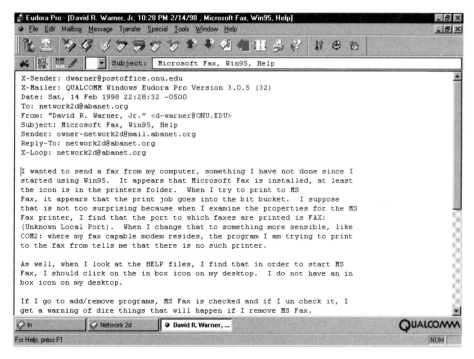

FIGURE 6-1. Network2d (formally named network2d-l) is an unmoderated list focusing on technology use in the law office. It is affiliated with *Network 2d,* the newsletter of the ABA's Law Practice Management Section Computer and Technology Interest Groups.

Finding Appropriate Mailing Lists

There are many legal-related mailing lists, and they are easy to find. The mother lode of legal-related mailing list information is the Law Lists site maintained by Lyonette Louis-Jacques at the University of Chicago Law School. For general information on the Law Lists, point your browser to:

http://www.lib.uchicago.edu/~llou/lawlists/info.html

To search for a mailing list by keyword, see:

http://www.lib.uchicago.edu/cgi-bin/law-lists

Each entry includes information about the list and how to subscribe. Other sources for mailing list information include the following:

♦ Mailing lists sponsored by the American Bar Association at http://www.abanet.org/discussions

FIGURE 6-2. On Lyonette Louis-Jacques's Law Lists Web site, you can search for legal-specific mailing lists.

- ◆ Regent University Law School's law-related LISTSERVs, which includes information on LISTSERV basics and Netiquette, at
  http://www.regent.edu/lawlib/lists/list-law.html

- ◆ LegalMinds, an archive of many public-interest mailing lists, provided by FindLaw at
  http://www.legalminds.org/

- ◆ LawGuru.Com's Mailing List Manager, which provides a forms-based method of subscribing, unsubscribing, and sending commands to more than five hundred mailing lists, at
  http://www.lawguru.com/subscribe/listtool.html

- ◆ The Liszt, which catalogues mailing lists of all types (not just legal ones), at
  http://www.liszt.com/

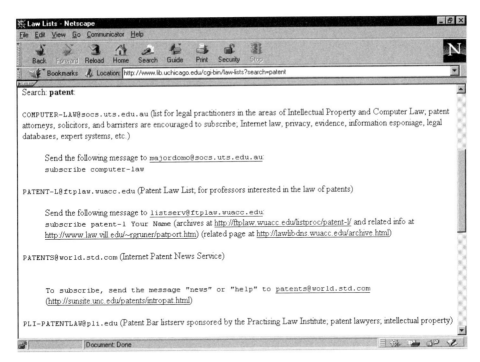

FIGURE 6-3. The Law Lists can be searched by keyword. This search shows mailing lists relating to patents.

Subscribing to Mailing Lists

Mailing lists have two addresses: (1) an administrative address that handles the subscription matters (i.e., subscribing and unsubscribing) and (2) a list address where all e-mail is sent. To subscribe, you send a message to the administrative address indicating the list to which you want to subscribe, for example, subscribe network2d.

Some lists also require you to send your real name, and they may require you to identify yourself if there is a prerequisite to joining (e.g., if the list is just for lawyers, you would have to say you're a lawyer or a judge). Still other lists may require you to reply to a welcome message before you're fully subscribed, just to ensure that you are really there. Here are three examples of popular legal mailing lists and their subscription messages.

Net-lawyers is a discussion list for those interesting in sharing information about using the Internet in research and the practice of law. To subscribe, send a message to

listserv@lawlib.wuacc.edu

with the following in the body of the message:

subscribe net-lawyers firstname lastname

(where, of course, *firstname lastname* is your real name).

Solosez is an ABA-sponsored mailing list for lawyers practicing solo or in small firms (i.e., five or fewer lawyers). To subscribe, send a message to

listserver@abanet.org

with the following message:

subscribe solosez

Law-lib focuses on issues related to law libraries and librarians. To subscribe, send a message to

listproc@ucdavis.edu

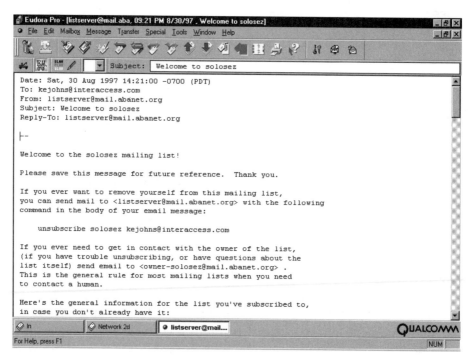

FIGURE 6-4. The welcoming message from the solosez mailing list includes information on how to unsubscribe and how to get help, as well as general information about the list.

with the following message:

`subscribe law-lib firstname lastname`

When subscribing to a mailing list, these are some points to keep in mind:

- **Leave the subject line blank.** A subject is not necessary. A computer is the only one that is reading your message. If your e-mail program requires that you enter a subject, just type in the word "subscribe."
- **Include only the subscription text in the message.** Anything else will generate an error message back to you because the mailing list software can't interpret it. (Usually, though, the subscription request will be accepted.)
- **Omit your signature line.** It also will usually generate an error.
- **Keep your welcoming message.** This will give you information on how to obtain help, where to find frequently asked questions, and more importantly, how to unsubscribe. Save this message in a separate folder, perhaps one just for mailing list administrative messages.

Getting Help (and Getting Out)

You can fine-tune your use of a mailing list by sending different administrative commands to the mailing list program. Many of these will be listed in the initial welcome message you receive from the program. Alternatively, you can send the list program mail with the word "help" alone in the message text (and again, no signature line).

Different mailing list programs offer different options, so get help instructions for each mailing list to which you subscribe and save each for future reference.

If you want to get off a mailing list, send an unsubscribe message to the mailing list administrative address, generally in the same format in which you subscribed, with the word "unsubscribe" and the list name. Remember that your welcome message will give instructions for unsubscribing.

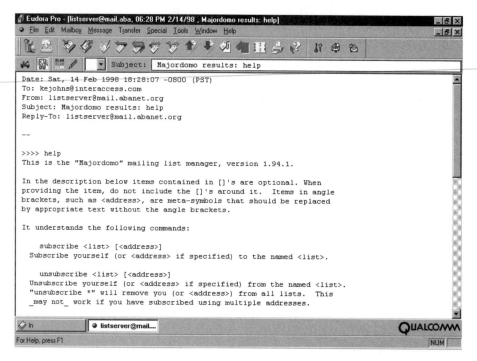

FIGURE 6-5. Here is returned help information from the network2d mailing list, sent by the Majordomo mailing list manager.

Sending and Receiving Messages from the List

As mentioned, mailing lists have an administrative address and a list distribution address. For example, my network2d mailing list has an administrative address of **listserver@abanet.org** and a list address (where the mail goes) of **network2d@abanet.org**.

Make sure not to confuse the two. Sending administrative messages like unsubscribe requests to the list address, where everyone sees (and probably comments on) your mistake, is a good way to get flamed.

Mailing lists may require you to send messages to the list from the same mail account under which you subscribed. Otherwise your messages will be rejected because you aren't recognized as a subscriber to the list. If you change mail accounts, you should unsubscribe from the old address and resubscribe from the new one.

Since mailing lists can generate a lot of messages, it is probably a bad idea to subscribe to several at once—you could get swamped with several hundred messages the first day. Filters are a good way to manage mailing lists. Create filters for each list, and put the messages in their own folders. That keeps your Inbox tidy (meaning there's less chance you'll overlook an important message) and also keeps all the list messages together so it's easier to see the message threads. Remember to delete old mailing list messages in these folders periodically, since otherwise they take up disk space.

Another way to cut down on the number of mailing list messages is the digest option. With this option individual messages are combined into a single digest message before sending. Check the help feature to see if your mailing list has a digest option.

Want to start your own mailing list? First check the Law Lists to see if an existing list covers the topics in which you are interested. If not, you can check with your ISP to see if it supports mailing lists. Many college and university computer systems also host mailing lists, as do bar associa-

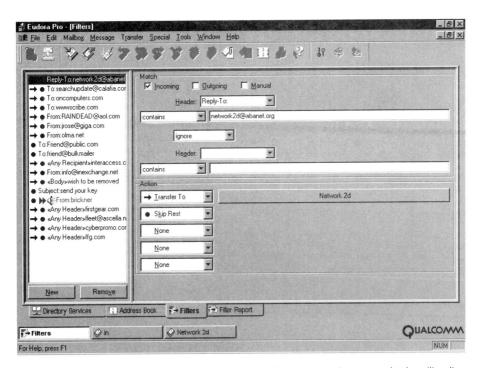

FIGURE 6-6. This Eudora filter will automatically transfer any incoming network2d mailing list messages from the Inbox to a special network2d mailbox.

tions like the ABA. Lastly, if you don't anticipate too many subscribers, you can easily do a mailing list by setting up the subscriber names in a group entry in your Address Book. When you are ready to do a mailing, just select that group address and your message will be distributed to the entire group.

Observing List Netiquette (and More Flame Avoidance)

Mailing lists have developed their own specialized Netiquette, beyond the "standard" e-mail Netiquette discussed in Chapter 3. These are the communal rules:

- **Use the right address.** Administrative messages (e.g., unsubscribe, help) go to the mailing list program, not to the distribution address. (Have I mentioned this enough?)
- **Get a feel for the list first.** After you subscribe, start reading messages but wait a few days before you send a message. This allows you to get a feel for the tone and flow of the list, get familiar with the people who do the postings, and see what topics interest (or bore) the subscribers.
- **Make sure the message is appropriate.** Your message should be relevant to the topic of the list. Don't ask a detailed intellectual property question of a list on immigration law.
- **Watch your reply.** Most list messages will go back to the list when you hit the reply button, but in some systems they go directly to the author (and not the list). Make sure the reply is going where you intend.
- **Personal messages should go to the individual, not the list.** If you want to send a personal reply to the author of a message and that reply isn't appropriate for everyone on the list to see, be *sure* to put the author's address in the To field and *take out* the list address. Even if your message is not personal, some things simply don't need to be sent to everyone.
- **Quote diligently.** In a reply, quote only enough of the original message to make your response understandable. Because of the volume of list mail, mailing list participants are not very tolerant of bloated messages with large amounts of irrelevant quoted text.
- **Consider that a large audience is reading your messages.** The audience could possibly include your present or future boss or present or future clients. Accordingly, take care in what you write. Mailing

list messages are frequently archived—what you say may be stored for a very long time in a place where people can get to it.

- **Assume that individuals speak for themselves.** Don't assume that people speak for their organizations (unless they explicitly say so). In their signature line some people include something similar to "these views are my own and do not reflect the views of ...."

- **Use a relevant subject line.** The subject line should correctly reflect the topic of the message. Messages get threaded and along the way sometimes have their content changed. If this happens, change the subject accordingly. It's courteous to show that the thread is moving in another direction. Use something like "Re: Windows Palmtops (was: case management tools)" or "Re: WAS Techshow, NOW WordPerfect vs. Word."

- **State it's Long if it's long.** If you are sending long messages, say more than two hundred lines, recipients will appreciate it if you include "-Long" in the subject line. This allows them to skip over the message if they're pressed for time.

- **Get the author's permission before posting.** If you've received a personal message that you want to post to a mailing list, get permission from the original author. Give proper attribution, even if you shorten the message or otherwise quote only the relevant parts.

- **Don't post ads.** The vast majority of mailing lists prohibit (explicitly or implicitly) the posting of advertisement messages. Nothing will get you flamed faster.

- **Don't cross-post.** Sending the same message to multiple mailing lists is considered bad form. Many people subscribe to multiple mailing lists (like you do), and they don't care to see the same message several times in multiple threads. If you really think the message is appropriate for more than one list, put "cross-posted to *listname*" at the beginning of the text to let people know they could see it again.

- **Don't take the bait.** Some messages are sent for no other reason than to generate controversy and possibly (hopefully?) to start a flame war. In the legal technology area, top subjects for starting arguments are Macintosh versus Windows, Word versus WordPerfect, and Microsoft versus the world. Don't get suckered into responding.

- **Don't send long messages if the information is available in another place.** If a significant court opinion is released on the Web, it makes little sense to copy the text into an e-mail message and send it to everyone on the list. Instead, simply send the Web site's URL in the message. Most current e-mail software will recognize a URL in a message and convert it into a true hypertext link. Click on it with the mouse, and the mail program will launch your Web browser and take you to that site.

◆ **Don't send attachments.** Rarely, if ever, does everyone on the list need to receive a file from you. It only makes people angry when they have to wait to download a file in which they have absolutely no interest. It also clogs up hard drives and possibly increases virus risks. (So what's an attachment? It's covered in the next chapter.)

Mailing lists are an excellent use of e-mail, allowing you to find other lawyers with similar interests, to get assistance when you need it, to stay current on legal developments, and to fulfill your continuing education. There's a lot of good information out there waiting for you—free and available for direct delivery to your desktop.

CHAPTER **SEVEN**

Sending More Than Text

IT'S NOT JUST FOR TEXT ANYMORE. One powerful feature of e-mail is the ability to send documents, presentations, spreadsheets, or any type of binary file along with an e-mail message. A binary file is a computer-readable file that most programs create. If you tried to read one of these files in a word processing program, it wouldn't make sense—you'd just see a bunch of jumbled characters. In contrast, ASCII files contain only text and numbers and are easily readable.

Binary files that are sent with e-mail messages are called "attachments." With attachments you can do many things, such as the following:

- ◆ Send a document draft to a client for review and editing.
- ◆ Distribute a firm newsletter in an electronic format such as Adobe Acrobat.
- ◆ Mail a database of contact information to a colleague who is traveling.
- ◆ Send a CLE presentation to the seminar's organizers.
- ◆ Send a voice mail as a sound file so your secretary can transcribe it.
- ◆ Receive program updates directly from the vendor via e-mail.

Attaching Files

The process of attaching a file to a message is simple. When you are composing a message, Eudora Pro, Netscape Messenger, and Microsoft Outlook Express all display a paper clip icon on the toolbar. (See Chapter 2 for an illustration.) Click on this icon, then select the file to attach from the files list. When you finish composing the message, send it as you normally would. The mail program will include the file with the message when the message is sent to the Internet.

Unfortunately, there's no guarantee that attached files will be received successfully. This is because of an inherent limitation in e-mail—and the ongoing evolution of a final standard for getting around that limitation.

Internet e-mail, built on sending ASCII text characters, cannot directly handle binary files. Hence, binary files are "encoded" into a series of ASCII characters, then put into the text of the message for sending. The

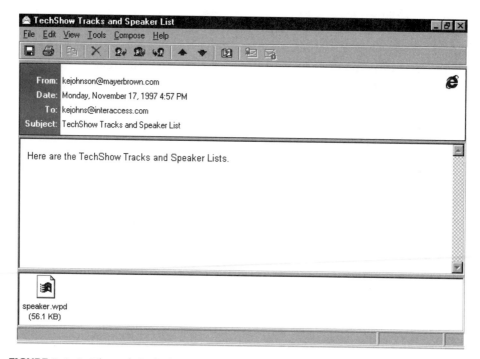

FIGURE 7-1. In Microsoft Outlook Express, a paper clip icon in the Inbox indicates an attachment. When reading the message, you double-click on the document icon at the bottom of the screen to open the attachment.

receiver's mail system must be able to decode the attachment back into its original binary file format. If the system cannot, the recipient ends up with a large amount of seemingly nonsense ASCII text.

There are three different encoding techniques used to attach files to e-mail messages: MIME, UUEncode, and BinHex. MIME, which stands for Multipurpose Internet Mail Extensions, is the most commonly used in current e-mail software and is the default for Eudora Pro, Netscape Messenger, and Microsoft Outlook Express.

Mail software will automatically encode files when you attach them to a message, so there is little you need to do other than specify the file name. When a message with an attachment is received, the mail program attempts to decode it. If it's successful, you'll see an indication of an attachment in the Inbox. Eudora shows a generic document icon (in version 3.0) or a paper clip icon (in version 4.0) in the attachment column. Outlook Express shows a paper clip icon. Netscape Messenger displays the attachment information when the file is opened.

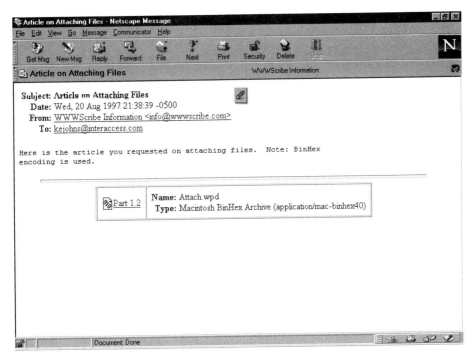

FIGURE 7-2. In Netscape Messenger, opening a message with an attachment brings up an attachment icon and information about the attachment method and the file's name.

Handling Attachments

When you receive an attachment, there will be an icon in the message to indicate that a file is attached. You generally have the option of opening or saving the attachment. (Take heed: "Opening" an executable file will run the program.) In Netscape Messenger and Outlook Express the attachment is stored as part of the message, but in Eudora Pro the file is physically placed in a directory on your hard drive (specified in Eudora Pro's Options).

In Eudora Pro, since the file is already stored in a download directory, you can access the attachment without even reading the accompanying message. To view the attachment from within Eudora Pro, double-click on the icon at the bottom on the message. Eudora will open the file, based on the program associated with the file's extension.

In Netscape Messenger, you double-click on the attachment icon. Netscape will prompt you (with a security warning message) to open the file or save it. If you merely want to save the attachment, the quick way is to right-click on the attachment and select Save Link As.

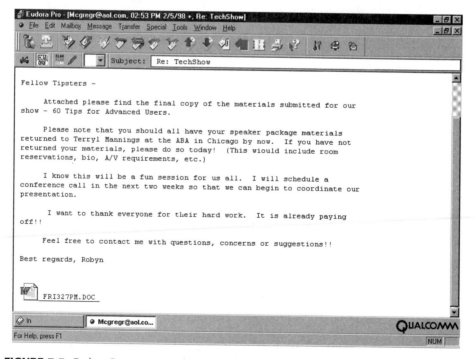

FIGURE 7-3. Eudora Pro stores attachments in a download directory, so there is no need to save the file from within a message. Double-click on the icon or the file name to open the file.

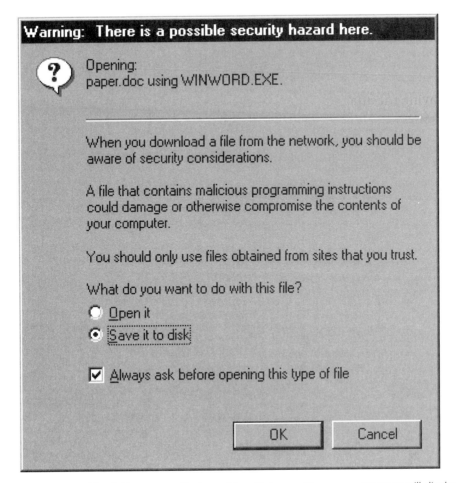

FIGURE 7-4. Double-clicking on an attachment in a Netscape Messenger message will display this warning screen, where you can choose to open the file with the associated application or save it to disk. Outlook Express works similarly.

Microsoft Outlook Express is similar to Netscape Messenger in handling attachments. You double-click on the icon, then elect to open or save from the resulting window. To save the attachment, right-click and select Save As.

Avoiding Attachment Pitfalls

The three different encoding techniques can cause headaches if the sender's and the receiver's mail systems don't use the same method. Clients don't like getting random ASCII text in a message when they were expecting a Word document, and they are likely to blame you rather than their antiquated mail program. Certainly, if you are on deadline and expecting something from a co-counsel, you don't want to get an attachment that you can't decode. So follow a few simple rules:

- ◆ **A successful attachment doesn't matter if what you send is unreadable.** Even if the attachment works, make sure that the person on the other end can actually use that file you've sent. Sending a Word 97 file to a client using DOS WordPerfect 5.1 is, even if it is decoded correctly, of little value. Likewise, receiving a Macintosh Aldus Persuasion file when your office is running Windows 3.1 won't be of much use. So part of your initial testing should be to make sure that both sides have the software to use the files that are being exchanged. Because of the variety of programs that you and your clients may be using, a couple of the "lowest common denominator" file formats can help in the exchange of files. One is RTF, for Rich Text Format, which carries some formatting and can be read by most Windows and Macintosh word processors. HTML files can be viewed in any Web browser. Of course, don't forget good old ASCII text, which almost any program can easily read.
- ◆ **Test first, *before* it's urgent.** Before you are facing a deadline and it is critical, do a test attachment. Send a small document (one or two pages) and see what encoding technique works successfully.
- ◆ **Try MIME first.** Since MIME is the most common attachment method, try it first (if you have an option of which encoding technique to use). If the recipient can't handle MIME, use BinHex for Macintosh users and UUEncode for DOS and Windows users.
- ◆ **If all else fails, use text.** When you can't get attachments to work with a recipient but you must send a document, save the document as ASCII text and put it into the body of the e-mail message. You'll lose formatting (and things like headers and footers), but at least you can get the words sent.

The Somewhat Gory Details of Attachments

For the most part you don't have to worry about encoding techniques and decoding attachments because the e-mail program handles them automatically. Occasionally, however, you may need to attach a file using a different method (perhaps the client's e-mail can only handle BinHex) or to deal with an attachment that didn't decode automatically. For those cases, here are the moderately complicated details.

Encoding and Decoding

The three major encoding schemes in use today are BinHex, UUEncode, and MIME. As mentioned at the beginning of the chapter, whatever you use to encode the attachment, the recipient must use the same to decode it.

- **MIME** is the most common encoding technique in current e-mail software. Unfortunately, some older e-mail programs don't support MIME. If you receive a MIME attachment that hasn't been decoded, it is easy to recognize by special headers at the beginning of the attachment indicating the MIME version and content type.
- **UUEncode,** and its companion UUDecode, were the early standards for encoding messages in the DOS and Windows worlds. An undecoded UUEncoded message will display the ASCII text bracketed with "begin" and "end" lines, with the original file name on the "begin" line.

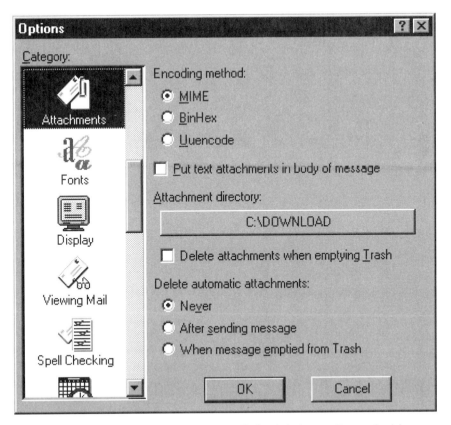

FIGURE 7-5. Eudora Pro Attachment Options specify the default encoding method, but you can select any of the others from the toolbar when creating the message. Here you also specify where you want the decoded files to be stored.

♦ **BinHex** is the UUEncode of the Macintosh world. An undecoded BinHex message begins with the text "This file must be converted with BinHex 4.0."

Eudora Pro, Microsoft Outlook Express, and Netscape Messenger support automatic decoding of all three types of attachments. Outlook Express and Netscape Messenger each attach messages using MIME, though Messenger lets you choose UUEncode on the Message Sending Options tab when creating a message. In Eudora Pro you can select the encoding method for each message from the toolbar, though one type is the default. Eudora Light supports MIME and BinHex but not UUEncode.

Manual Decoding

If you receive attachments in a method that your mail program does not support, all is not lost. Several manual decoding programs are available on the Internet and through CompuServe and AOL.

Wincode, written by G.H. Silva, is a popular freeware Windows encoder and decoder that handles UUEncode, MIME, and BinHex. Wincode supports drag and drop and handles single and multiple-part encoded files. Wincode is available at

http://www.pcworld.com/software_lib/data/articles/internet/1770.html

ESS-Code, from Electric Storm Software, handles UUEncode and MIME attachments. Versions of ESS-Code are available for Windows, Windows 95/NT, and DOS. ESS-Code offers a Wizard feature to help decode (and encode) files, or you can decode and encode by selecting the appropriate encoding type from the File menu. ESS-Code is available at

http://www6.zdnet.com/cgi-bin/texis/swlib/hotfiles/info.html?fcode=00064M
(for Windows 3.1)

http://www6.zdnet.com/cgi-bin/texis/swlib/hotfiles/info.html?fcode=0001LZ
(for Windows 95)

Another program, InterCode for Windows (ICODE), by Jeff Lee, handles UUEncode, MIME, and BinHex. It features automatic detection of encoding type, handles multipart encoded files, does background decoding, and supports drag and drop. It also includes automatic detection and special handling of files split when being sent from AOL. ICODE is available at

http://www.powerconcorp.com/info/utils/icode300.zip

The ability to share files is a great feature of e-mail, though it may take some effort to get the mail programs at both ends to work together to encode and decode the files successfully. The key point is to test and get the procedure down before a crisis hits.

*CHAPTER***EIGHT**

Dealing with Security, Encryption, and Ethics Concerns

THE SECURITY OF E-MAIL MESSAGES is a big topic on the Internet—and one that particularly concerns lawyers. As discussed previously, Internet e-mail is not secure. Your messages can readily be read by your firm's or the ISP's systems administrator, if they're so moved. The channels over which your messages travel are not physically secure, so snoopers can access them. E-mail storage on your ISP's network isn't necessarily protected. Pretty frightening, isn't it? Well, there is good news.

The huge volume of traffic on the Internet realistically means that there's little chance that someone is going to tap into your messages. However, a chance still exists. Fortunately, for true confidentiality messages can by encrypted so that only the intended recipient can read the contents. (Everyone else would just see garbage text).

Understanding Security Considerations

Before delving into encryption methods, it's important to understand the range of e-mail security concerns. Encrypting messages doesn't do much good if you leave other security holes open. Here are key considerations:

- **E-mail is most likely to be compromised from your own computer.** This includes e-mail printouts being taken from (or read at) a printer. Don't print confidential messages if you can't be standing there as the paper comes out of the printer. Protect the physical security of your computer. Someone could open your e-mail and read your messages. In addition, e-mail messages can be opened directly off the hard drive, since they are stored in plain-text files. Even deleted messages might be read. For example, in Eudora, when you delete a message from a mailbox, it still exists in a file on your hard drive—until you "compact" the mailbox and it finally is physically deleted from the hard drive.

- **Watch your password.** Don't save your password in your e-mail program or Internet access software, *especially* on a laptop. Keep your password safe and change it frequently. A password should not be a common word, certainly not one in the dictionary. (To break into systems, hackers use a program that tries all the words in the dictionary.) The best passwords are a combination of letters and numbers or symbols.

- **The biggest security risk comes from insiders.** This includes disgruntled or dismissed employees. When people leave your firm, disable their logon I.D. (if on a network) or physically secure their computers before they leave the building.

- **Protect your laptop.** A stolen or lost laptop can lead to disaster. Someone could read all your documents, print your client list, and review all your e-mail. Put a boot-up password on your laptop. This requires that the password be entered whenever you turn on the laptop or all access will be prevented—including booting up from a floppy disk. Specifying a boot-up password is done though the laptop's setup program.

- **Consider incorrectly delivered mail.** Watch your addressing. Make a mistake and your message could go to a different person at the correct domain, or to the wrong person at the wrong domain (e.g., if you picked the wrong name from your Address Book). The problem is that these messages do get delivered, so you don't know you've sent the message to the wrong person, unless the person replies with something like, "Why did you send me this message?"

- ◆ **You have no control over what the recipient does with your message.** Your message can be forwarded to someone even though you never intended for that person to see it. It can be forwarded to a mailing list, where a *whole lot* of people would see it despite your intentions. Your words can be edited and sent on as "original" quoted text from you. Even if you encrypt a message, the recipient can decrypt it and pass it along in its unencrypted form.

Encryption is the only real way to ensure security of e-mail between yourself and the recipient. When you encrypt a message, based on a "key," it is rendered into a seemingly random set of letters, numbers, and symbols. Anyone who wrongly intercepts the message sees only junk text. The intended recipient uses the key to turn that junk back into intelligible text. One popular encryption technology for e-mail is PGP.

Encrypting for Pretty Good Privacy

PGP, meaning Pretty Good Privacy, was developed by Philip Zimmermann, a true hero of Internet users. Like the name says, PGP is pretty good security—in fact, it's a high level of security if used correctly. PGP is

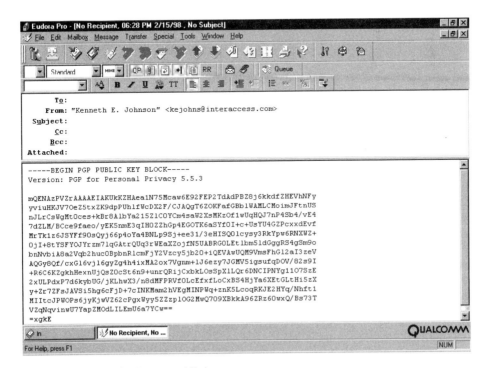

FIGURE 8-1. The author's PGP public key.

based on a "public key" encryption technique, which uses two complementary keys to secure messages. You have a public key and a private key. Your recipient will need your public key, but it makes no difference who else has it. (By the way, no one can determine your private key based on your public one.)

Keys are kept in special files called "key rings." Your private key is protected by a passphrase (i.e., password), which must be entered to use the key. You can distribute your public key in several ways:

- Include it in an e-mail to parties who want to exchange secured messages with you, since the key is simply a text string. They then include your key in their key ring.
- Place your key on a public key server. Here someone can search for and get a copy of your key, without explicitly having to ask for a copy.
- Put a copy of your key on your Web site.
- Define a filter that will automatically reply to someone with your key. In Eudora, for example, you could set this up to look for "send

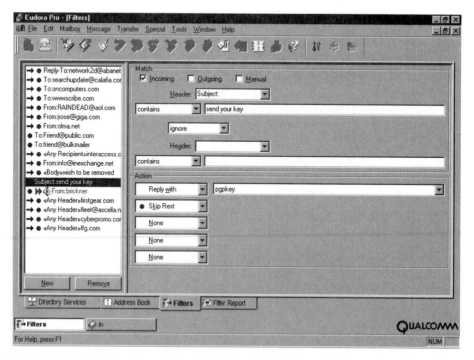

FIGURE 8-2. This Eudora filter will automatically reply with the author's PGP key when someone sends a message with "send your key" in the subject line.

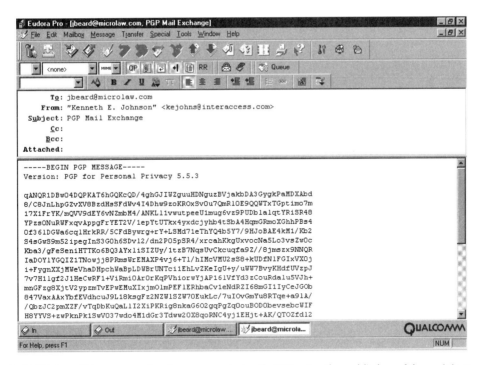

FIGURE 8-3. This message has been encrypted with PGP using the public key of the recipient, who is the only one who can decipher it.

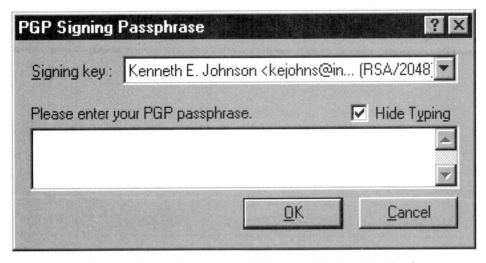

FIGURE 8-4. When you digitally sign a message, it lets the recipient confirm that the message came from you and has not been altered. Signing is done with your private key and so requires that you enter your passphrase for access.

your key" in the subject line, then to reply with a template message containing your key.

When you want to send secure e-mail, you use the recipients' public key to encrypt the message. They then use their private key to decipher the information. Likewise, someone wanting to send you secure e-mail uses your public key to encrypt, and you decrypt using your private key.

PGP also offers digital signatures, which allow you to indicate that the message truly came from you and is complete and unaltered. You "sign" a message using your private key. The recipient uses his or her copy of your public key to check the contents of the message to ensure that no one has tampered with the contents. If the check passes, then your message was not modified in transit.

Encoding and Decoding an E-mail Message

PGP was somewhat difficult to use in the past because it was not integrated with e-mail software. Messages had to be written in a text editor, saved as a file that was then encrypted, and attached to a message and sent. Now, however, PGP is becoming widely available as an e-mail software "plug-in," meaning it is integrated into the program. Encrypting and decrypting is done with a few mouse clicks on the appropriate PGP buttons.

Encoding a message with Eudora's PGP plug-in adds some steps to the sending process:

1. Create the message as you normally would. Remember that to send an encrypted message you must have the recipient's PGP public key; it needs to be in your key ring already.
2. Don't use a signature. In the current version of PGP for Eudora, the signature will cause the message to fail validation on the other end. Because Eudora adds a signature as the message is sent, it is added after the message is encoded or digitally signed. When the recipient gets the message, it will appear that it has been modified in transit.
3. Click on the envelope-lock icon to encrypt the message.
4. Click on the quill pen icon to sign the message digitally.
5. Send the message.
6. The PGP address list will open. Select the recipient's address, if it is not already filled in. This completes the encryption phase.
7. The PGP Signing Passphrase window will open if you've selected a digital signature. Enter the PGP password for your private key.
8. The message is now stored in the Outbox.

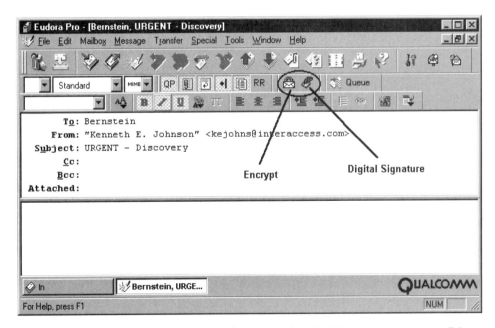

FIGURE 8-5. PGP for Personal Privacy is a plug-in to Eudora Pro. To encrypt a message, click on the envelope-lock icon on the toolbar. For your electronic signature, click on the quill pen icon.

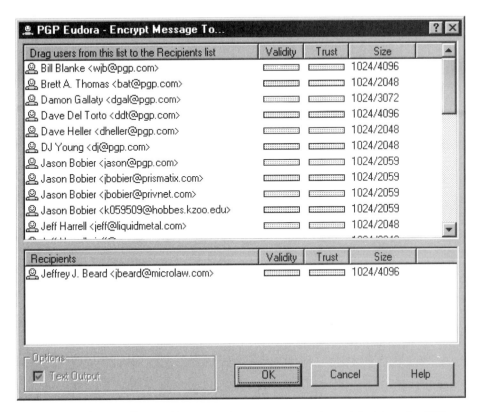

FIGURE 8-6. When sending a PGP-encrypted message, select the recipient from the PGP user list (a list of the people whose public key is on your key ring).

Decoding a PGP-encrypted message you've received takes fewer steps:

1. When you open the message, you'll see the PGP Message block and its scrambled text.
2. Click on the open envelope icon on the toolbar.
3. Enter your PGP passphrase.
4. The message is then decoded, and if it is digitally signed, you'll see a window showing whether the message is valid.

PGP is not without some vulnerabilities. The most obvious is that if someone learns your passphrase, they can access your private key and read encrypted messages to you and send signed messages as you. Protect your passphrase (don't write it down anywhere), and as with any password, don't use common words. Use multiple words but not common quotations or phrases, and include numbers or symbols. Public key tampering is also a possibility, as in someone substituting their public key with your user name so they get and can encrypt messages meant for you.

In addition, always remember that encryption works between you and the recipient. Once the recipient receives and decrypts the message, they can then send it on to anyone else in its plain-text state.

Another thing to consider is traffic analysis. Even if your messages are encrypted and can't be read, a snoop can learn much by analyzing where your messages come and go from, the size of the messages (big ones may be file attachments), the time of day messages are sent, and so forth. For example, tracking messages between your firm and domains can provide information about who is a client. A sudden flurry in messages may suggest something is happening with that client, perhaps an SEC filing, an upcoming indictment, an impending settlement, or the like.

PGP is an important addition to your e-mail if you're concerned with security—and what lawyer is not? While not necessary for every message,

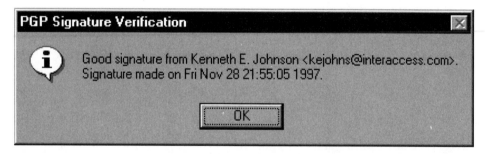

FIGURE 8-7. This message indicates that the digital signature was accepted and the message came from the correct person and has not been modified in transit.

FIGURE 8-8. The Pretty Good Privacy (PGP) Awareness Project, from The Computer Law Resource (**http://www.CompLaw.com/pgp.html**), provides PGP information designed for lawyers.

there are certainly times when sending encrypted e-mail is important. (For more information on PGP, see the online resources in Appendix D.)

Using Digital Certificates

Both Netscape Messenger and Microsoft Outlook Express implement security by way of a security standard known as S/MIME, or Secure MIME. Personal digital certificates store your key information and are used to sign messages and send encrypted mail. These certificates are issued by third-party certificate authorities, such as VeriSign. At VeriSign's Web site, you can obtain a signature and it will be automatically downloaded and installed in your browser and e-mail programs.

Encryption and signatures work in very much the same way as PGP public and private keys do. When a secure message is sent, part of the recipient's digital certificate is used to encrypt the message; the recipient then uses another part of his or her certificate to decrypt it. Digital signatures work similarly.

FIGURE 8-9. VeriSign provides digital signatures to individuals for use with Netscape Messenger and Microsoft Outlook Express. There are different levels of certificates, available at different costs.

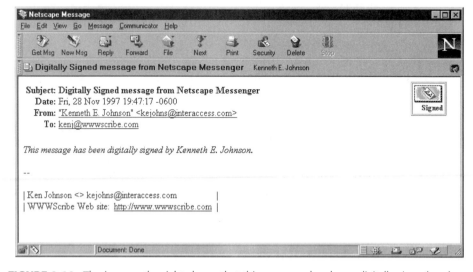

FIGURE 8-10. The icon on the right shows that this message has been digitally signed and validated. Double-clicking on the icon brings up specific security information.

A Word about Ethics Opinions on Encrypted E-mail

Ethics discussions are underway in many states regarding encrypting e-mail and the duty to maintain confidentiality. For example, the Illinois State Bar Association Advisory Opinion on Professional Conduct, Opinion No. 96-10, says that lawyers may use e-mail without encryption to communicate with clients unless "unusual circumstances require enhanced security measures." Iowa, on the other hand, issued an opinion (Opinion 95-30) stating that lawyers must encrypt sensitive material before sending it via e-mail, but this was amended (Opinion 97-10) to allow unencrypted e-mail if the client acknowledges the risk in writing.

It is important that you stay in contact with your state bar's ethics committee regarding ruling on these matters. Summaries of states' ethics opinions are available at LegalEthics.Com at

http://www.legalethics.com/states.htm

LegalEthics.Com includes links to several articles on e-mail and confidentiality, including the following:

- "Client Confidentiality: A Lawyer's Duties with Regard to Internet E-mail," by Robert L. Jones (http://www.computerbar.org/netethics/bjones.htm).
- "E-mail and the Attorney-Client Privilege," by Arthur Smith (http://www.abelaw.com/bamsl/lpm/email.htm).
- "Professional Responsibility and Confidentiality Considerations When Using the Internet," by Mary Frances Lapidus (http://www.legalethics.com/articles/lapidus1.htm).
- "E-mail: How Attorneys Are Changing the Way They Communicate," by Susan B. Ross, which discusses some practical and ethical issues associated with e-mail use by lawyers (http://www.collegehill.com/ilp-news/ross-email.html).
- "Internet Communications, Part II, A Larger Perspective" (originally published in *ALAS Loss Prevention Journal*), by William Freivogel, which discusses the issue of Internet communications encryption (http://www.legalethics .com/articles/freivogel.htm).

Addressing the Legal and Ethical Issues of E-mail

A final point to consider, which is definitely not the least important topic in this book, is the ethical and legal issues of e-mail. Like any document, e-mail messages can be subject to discovery, subpoena, and admittance into evidence in a trial. They can also get you, your firm, and your clients into trouble. (Conversely, if you are doing discovery, failing to request e-mail messages may cause you to miss many relevant facts for your case.) Because of the medium's less-formal nature, e-mail writers are not as careful in the substance and format of e-mail messages. They may be freer with inappropriate or defamatory comments than in casual conversation.

These issues are compounded by the fact that e-mail can exist for a long time, and as such it can rear its ugly head long after it was written. E-mail can sit on hard drives and backup tapes for months or years. Even "deleted" messages can often be recovered from a hard drive by specialists. Quite a few supposedly erased e-mail messages have turned up in court cases.

As a general guideline, delete e-mail messages after a short, specified period of time (e.g., thirty to sixty days), and never archive e-mail on backup tapes. E-mail was never intended to be a permanent record. If you need to keep a message, print it out and file it or save it as a text file or in a document or database.

Every organization should have a formal policy on e-mail use. These policies often include the following:

- An explanation of the proper business usage of the e-mail system, and the level of personal use (if any) that is acceptable.
- A directive not to violate copyright laws by sending or printing copyrighted materials.
- A statement that sending offensive materials, solicitations, or chain letters and conducting illegal activities through e-mail are not permitted and will not be tolerated.
- A statement that messages may be maintained for some period, and even deleted messages may be recoverable.
- A statement that the organization has the right to monitor e-mail and disclose e-mail communications if necessary.

A law firm's e-mail use policy might also include the following:

- A notice that because substantial legal issues are discussed by e-mail, lawyers should promptly review their e-mail and make arrangements to have their mail read if they are away from the office or do not use a computer.
- Firm policies for e-mail security and encryption, and a statement on whether these may affect the retention policy.

◆ Security procedures for traveling outside of the office with a laptop and for checking e-mail remotely.

An e-mail policy, which may be part of a larger Internet use policy, should be in writing, signed by all employees, and kept on file. Such a policy should also state the penalties for violations of the policy.

*CHAPTER*NINE

Conclusion

FEW LAWYERS CAN AFFORD TO BE WITHOUT E-MAIL, for the most basic reason that clients are increasingly demanding that their lawyers be reachable online. If your clients aren't demanding it yet, they probably will—and sooner than later. So use your e-mail availability in marketing your practice, although that is certainly not the only reason to use e-mail.

This book has discussed a number of e-mail's benefits. It's practically free if you already have and use an Internet connection. Messages can be transmitted around the world in a matter of minutes, with no concern for distance and time zones. A single message can be sent to one person or to many and, in the case of mailing lists, to hundreds at once. Replies can include the text of the original message to provide context. Files can be attached to messages for easy exchange of work product with clients and colleagues.

In addition, mailing lists are an excellent way to use e-mail to improve your lawyering skills. You can communicate with like-minded colleagues, learn more about what's new in your practice area, obtain help for various types of problems, contribute your expertise, and go off on a few interesting tangents. Finding a legal mailing list to match your interests is simple—just point your Web browser to Lyonette Louis-Jacques's Law List at http://www.lib.uchicago.edu/cgi-bin/law-lists.

Getting started with e-mail is an easy process. If you have Netscape Communicator 4.0, Netscape Navigator 3.0, or Microsoft Internet Explorer 3.0 or 4.0, you already have an e-mail program. Alternatively, you

may want to purchase a program like Eudora Pro, which has more features than the Netscape and Microsoft mail programs (e.g., sophisticated
filtering, multiple signatures, and a PGP add-on). Once you install and
configure your e-mail program, you are ready to start sending and receiving e-mail with a few clicks of the mouse.

When you're set up and using e-mail in your practice, drop me a line
at kejohns@interaccess.com and let me know how you're doing.

APPENDIX **A**

Learning More

Sending and receiving messages, keeping in touch with clients, collaborating with your colleagues through mailing lists, and sending documents to clients for review are all fundamental uses of Internet e-mail. Whether you're an e-mail novice or an experienced user, knowledge of a few additional topics is also helpful. What do those occasional error messages mean? How does a customized data delivery service work? What about these e-mail virus warnings I get? Is there any response to junk e-mail messages that flood my Inbox?

Mail Errors

When an e-mail message comes back to you with an error, it's called a "bounce" (as in "the message bounced back"). There are three typical reasons why e-mail bounces:

Host Unknown. This indicates that the mail system can't find the recipient's domain. Check the spelling of the domain name, and make sure that the domain name is complete. Remember the different top-level domain names: com, org, net, edu, and so forth.

Domain names usually have some relationship to the "real" name of the organization to which you're e-mailing, but it might not be what you think. Considering sending e-mail to someone at the American Bar Association? The ABA's domain name is abanet.org. It's not aba.com (American Banking Association) or aba.net (American Business Owners Association) or aba.org (American Birding Association).

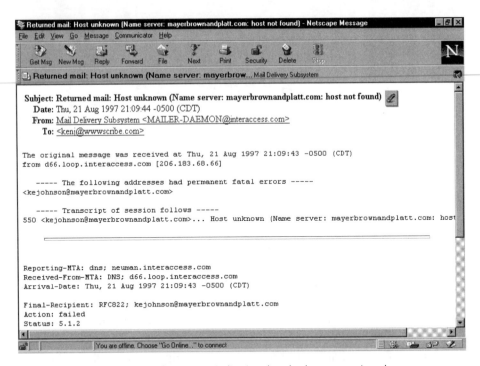

FIGURE A-1. This is a bounced message indicating that the host name is unknown.

User Unknown. This indicates that the user account cannot be found on the domain. Again, check the name and the domain spelling. You may have misspelled the name, or correctly spelled the name but used the wrong domain name.

Mail Cannot Be Delivered. Your e-mail is trying to get there, but the mail server is not receiving mail. It could be that the network sending the mail can't contact that mail server, the network of the mail server is down, or the mail server is not configured correctly. These messages will usually say that the attempted mail delivery will continue for a few days.

There is no standardized format for error messages, so examine each one closely to find out what the source of the error is.

Push Technology

Push technology is an Internet buzzword that refers to the delivery of customized data directly to your computer. Both the Netscape and Microsoft Web browsers have components for this feature—you sign up, you indicate your interests (e.g., company information, stock quotes, sports scores), and that information comes directly to your browser.

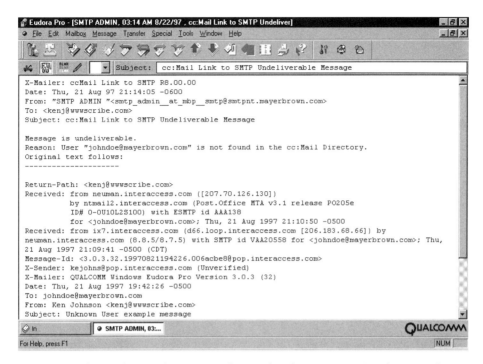

FIGURE A-2. This is a bounced message indicating that the user name is unknown at that domain.

Although it's not as "sexy" as some desktop delivery systems, e-mail can easily be used for receiving information you want. There are many services that you register with by giving your e-mail address. The news or material that you're interested in comes to you via e-mail at no charge. The services are often supported by advertisers, and a small advertisement or two is included in each mailing to you.

These are some examples of e-mail information delivery services:

- **WESTClip:** With this Westlaw service, searches can be saved, then rerun on a regular interval (e.g., daily, weekly, monthly), with the search results delivered to you via e-mail.
- **Lexis Eclipse:** Similar to WESTClip, your Lexis search results can be sent to you automatically by e-mail.
- **InfoBeat:** Formally known as Mercury Mail, this service gives stock, company, and Internet news, along with general news topics. Specify what material you want to receive, and when (e.g., closing bell versus morning edition), and each business day you receive e-mail with that information. InfoBeat is at **http://www.infobeat.com**.

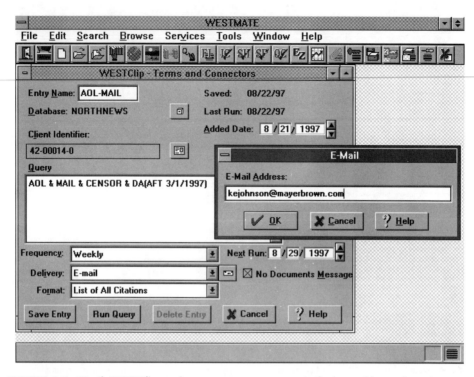

FIGURE A-3. West's WESTClip service can rerun your query at designated intervals and return the search results to you via e-mail.

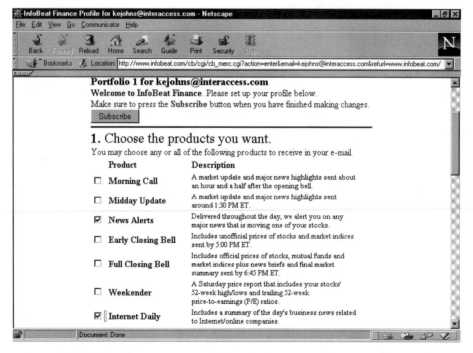

FIGURE A-4. InfoBeat offers a variety of information (here financial and company news) delivered regularly via e-mail.

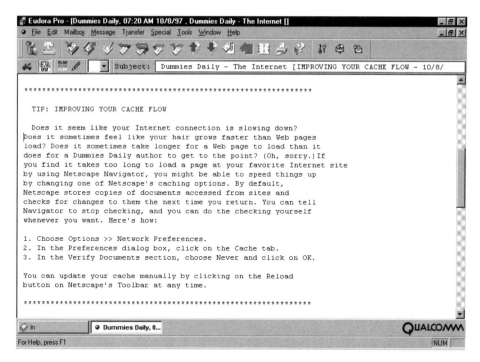

FIGURE A-5. This Internet tip was delivered by e-mail from the Dummies Daily Web site.

◆ **Dummies Daily:** A tip of the day is available from the "Dummies" book folks. Subjects include the Internet, the Web after 5:00, Microsoft Word 97, and Microsoft Excel 97. Register at http:// www.dummiesdaily.com.

What About Viruses?

Warnings are flying all over the Internet about e-mail messages that, if you open them, will wipe out your hard drive and do all kinds of other nasty things to your computer. These messages supposedly have subjects like "Good Times," "AOL4Free," and "Join the Crew." The warning comes to you (often with a lot of forwards) with the urgent request to forward it to everyone you know.

These messages are all hoaxes. They're the equivalent of scare chain letters. As mentioned in Chapter 7, e-mail messages are just ASCII text. Viruses cannot travel in text. They can only travel in executable programs (EXE and COM files) or in Word documents (the "virus" is part of the macro code in the DOC file). So it is simply impossible for a virus to infect your system by opening and reading an e-mail message.

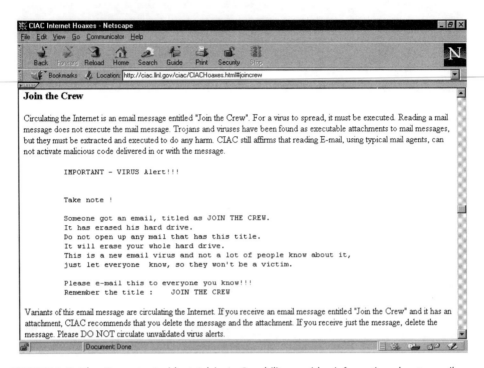

FIGURE A-6. The Computer Incident Advisory Capability provides information about e-mail virus hoaxes on its Web site.

If you get such a warning message, discard it. Don't forward it on and perpetuate the hoax—and needlessly scare others. Two tip-offs of hoaxes are technical-sounding jargon (which usually isn't correct) and an admonition to send a copy of the message to all your friends and acquaintances. Another red flag is if the message claims that the warning comes from the Federal Communications Commission—which does not distribute virus warnings.

The Department of Energy's Computer Incident Advisory Capability (CIAC) posts information about virus hoaxes on its Web site at

http://ciac.llnl.gov/ciac/CIACHoaxes.html

If you get a virus warning and are concerned, CIAC's site can give you the facts.

However, attachments can be a threat. If someone sends you an attached program, or Word document, you should always virus check the file before using it. Copy the attachment to a directory, and run your antivirus program against it. Obviously, it's also a good idea to know who sent the program or document to you. If something comes from out of the blue from an unknown source, the best idea is to delete the attachment immediately.

Spam, Spam, Spam, Spam . . .

Is your mailbox getting increasingly filled with junk e-mail messages? If not, it probably will. One of the worst aspects of the Internet is junk e-mail, commonly known as "spam" (after the Monty Python skit in which everyone kept singing, "Spam, spam, spam, spam, spam, spam, spam, spam").

Spam is unsolicited mail sent to hundreds, if not thousands, of users at once. Spam messages are usually advertisements for things you don't want, including "get rich quick" schemes, "lose weight fast" come-ons, invitations for adult services on the Internet, and programs to do spamming yourself. Often the messages carry subjects to make you think that the sender is someone you know (e.g., "See you tomorrow"), so you'll be sure to open the message.

Spam is worse than post office junk mail for a couple of reasons. It costs you money, since you have to download these messages and pay for the connection time to the mail server. You don't know it's junk until you read it. Most spammers hide their identity by sending out their junk using someone else's domain name as the return address, or even by accessing that person's mail server, so the spam cannot be traced back to them. One day this unlucky person could be you!

How do spammers get your e-mail address? The majority get addresses from America Online, CompuServe, and Prodigy forums and mailing lists. (AOL, in particular, sells its membership list, though it has policies against spam.) This is why you're more likely to receive junk at those addresses than at an e-mail address at an ISP. Your address could also be grabbed from postings that you make to newsgroups and mailing lists. It could be obtained by devious means from your ISP. It could be copied from your Web page.

So what can you do about spam?

Don't reply to the messages. The spammer has probably hidden its identity and the message will bounce back anyway.

Don't unsubscribe. Some spam will carry a statement that if you don't want to receive any additional messages, send a "remove" e-mail to a certain address. Don't do it. Sending a message shows that your e-mail account is active, and your address is sold to even more spammers.

Examine the message header. By reviewing the header, you can often determine what domain the spam came from, and what domains it

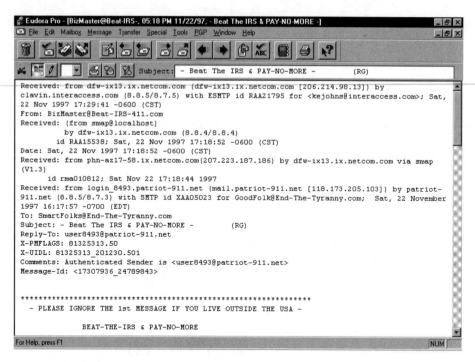

FIGURE A-7. The header of this spam message shows that the message seems to have originated at a domain called patriot-911.net and passed through the ix.netcom.com domain. (You read domains from bottom to top to see the path the message took.)

passed through. Display the full header of the message, then forward it (with a statement of your displeasure over receiving it) to

postmaster@*domain*
abuse@*domain*
spam@*domain*

Some of these might bounce back, but "postmaster" should always get through. Because of spam, some domains have set up special mail accounts for reporting spam at either "abuse" (the most common) or "spam."

You may or may not get a response back from the postmaster, but generally a postmaster will investigate. If the spammer is legitimately on that system, the spammer will either be warned or have its access terminated. (One of my claims to fame is getting a spammer thrown off of his ISP.) If the spammer used fraudulent message header information, at least the postmaster knows that the service is being misrepresented.

Send a copy (with full headers) to your ISP or online service. They can also investigate the abuse and possibly configure their system to reject messages from known spammers.

Filter. Use filters in your e-mail to dump spam automatically. For example, you could filter on "$$$," "!!!," or "make money fast" in the subject line. If you are repeatedly spammed from a particular domain, filter all mail from that domain name. Another option is to filter any messages not addressed specifically to you. Most spammers don't send directly to your address but instead use a list address to distribute the mail. So you can filter out any mail that doesn't have your address in the To field.

What should the filter do? Typically, you'd think it would just move the message to the Trash or Deleted Items folder and be done with it. Or with Eudora or Outlook Express, delete it from the server. However, take care that you will not get a legitimate message that meets the filtering criteria. A better strategy is to set up a "Spam" folder, or mailbox, and then direct all the messages there. Occasionally review the contents of the folder for any legitimate messages, and delete the rest. (This can

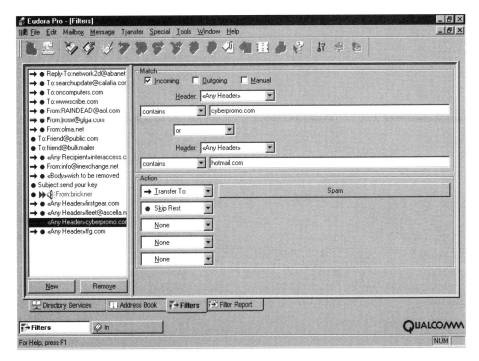

FIGURE A-8. This Eudora filter looks for spam messages from cyberpromo.com or hotmail.com and moves them to the Spam folder.

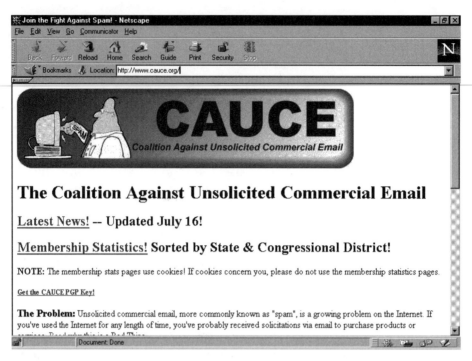

FIGURE A-9. The Coalition Against Unsolicited Commercial E-mail promotes amending 47 U.S.C. 227, the section of U.S. law that bans "junk faxing," to cover electronic mail.

usually be done by looking at the sender and subject, without having to open each message.)

Several organizations are working to lessen the amount of junk e-mail by adding unsolicited e-mail to the "junk fax" regulations. You can follow these activities online at the Coalition Against Unsolicited Commercial E-mail home page at http://www.cauce.org/.

APPENDIX **B**

E-mail Program Sources

There are a number of e-mail programs on the market. This book focuses on Eudora, Netscape Messenger, and Microsoft Outlook Express. Listed in this appendix are sources of information about these and other programs, along with where they can be downloaded.

About the URLs in This Book

First, a caveat about the URLs listed here and elsewhere in the book. The World Wide Web is anything but static, and Web documents are frequently changed, deleted, or moved to a different URL. If you try a URL and get an error message, back up one or two directories in the URL "path" and try again. Or, start at the topmost point, the domain name, and follow the links downward. For example, if you get an error trying to reach

http://www.microsoft.com/ie/sysreq.htm

then try

http://www.microsoft.com/ie

or the topmost level

http://www.microsoft.com

Eudora

http://www.eudora.com/eudoralight/download.html
    Download Eudora Light.

http://www.eudora.com/buying/qc.html
    Order Eudora Pro directly from Qualcomm.

Microsoft Outlook Express

http://www.microsoft.com/ie/download
    Download Microsoft's Internet Explorer, including Outlook Express.

http://www.microsoft.com/ie/ie40/download/addon.htm
    Download Outlook Express if you already have Internet Explorer 4.0
    installed.

Netscape Messenger

http://home.netscape.com/try/download/index.html
    Download Netscape Communicator and Netscape Navigator, includ-
    ing Internet E-mail.

Other E-mail Software

Pegasus Mail
http://www.pegasus.usa.com
    A free e-mail package for Windows 3.1, Windows 95, and Windows
    NT. Pegasus is very powerful but somewhat quirky and awkward to
    use—it is probably best suited for experienced e-mail users.

QuickMail Pro
http://www.cesoft.com
    A popular Macintosh e-mail program, now available for Windows 95
    and Windows NT. A trial version is available for downloading.

Z-Mail Pro
http://www.netmanage.com/products/hostlink97/zmail.html
    Another Windows 95 and Windows NT e-mail program, with a some-
    what cumbersome setup and interface—perhaps best suited for expe-
    rienced e-mail users. A trial version is available for downloading.

CyberCreek Mail
http://www.cybercreek.com

A popular e-mail program among teachers and schools, particularly since there is a free version available (CyberCreek Mail Express) for downloading.

Program Reviews

http://www.cnet.com/Content/Reviews/Compare/Emailclients/index.html

ClNet's review of seven e-mail packages, including Eudora, Netscape Messenger, Microsoft Outlook Express, Pegasus Mail, Pronto97, QuickMail Pro, and Z-Mail Pro.

APPENDIX C

Glossary of E-mail Terms

acceptable use policy A description of specific behavior allowed (and not allowed) by an ISP or online service. Most have policies against sending unsolicited bulk e-mail (or "spam").

address See **e-mail address**.

ASCII American Standard Code for Information Interchange. This is a "lowest common denominator" technique for exchanging data via simple text files (called ASCII files). ASCII files contain only the characters from a standard keyboard, as well as some generic, nonprinting formatting characters like tabs and carriage returns.

BFN E-mail abbreviation for "bye for now." Some also use BBFN, for "bye-bye for now."

binary file A file in computer-readable format consisting of a series of ones and zeros. The files saved in most software programs are binary files: word processing documents, spreadsheets, presentation graphics, and so on. This is in contrast to an ASCII file.

BinHex An attachment encoding/decoding technique used primarily on Macintosh systems.

bounce What an undelivered e-mail message does—that is, it bounces back to the sender. The sender is notified that the message did not get through and can check the bounced message to determine the reason for the problem: the domain cannot be found, the user is unknown at that domain, or the mail server involved is not receiving mail.

BTW   E-mail abbreviation for "by the way."

.com   Top-level domain that, as part of a domain name (e.g., abanet.com), indicates that the host computer is run by a commercial enterprise.

country code   As the last part of a domain name, indicates the country of the host computer. For example, the United States is **.us,** Canada is **.ca,** and Mexico is **.mx**. Most domain names do not include a country code.

daemon   A program that sits in the system background and (in this case) handles the transmitting of e-mail. If a mail message has an error and bounces back to you, you will receive a message from the daemon.

dial up   The process of calling another computer through the telephone lines. Dial-Up Networking in Microsoft Windows 95 provides access to the Internet.

digest   A compiled group of e-mail messages received in one big message. This is an option provided by some mailing lists, and it saves you from having to read (and deal with) a sizable group of individual messages.

digital signature   A means for providing authentication that a message was sent by the person whose name is on the message and that the message was not altered during sending. With PGP, you create a digital signature using your private key; the recipient validates the signature using your public key. In Netscape Messenger and Microsoft Outlook Express, digital signatures are created using certificates.

domain   The "natural language" name for a computer or network of computers on the Internet. Domain Name Services translates the domain name (e.g., mayerbrown.com) into the numeric IP address actually needed to contact that computer.

dot   Pronunciation of the period that appears in domain names. For example, the domain name mayerbrown.com is pronounced "Mayer Brown Dot Com."

e-mail   Abbreviation for electronic mail. Also sometimes spelled as **Email.**

e-mail address   The online address to which your electronic mail is delivered, consisting of your user name and the host computer handling the mail. The two parts are joined by the "at" sign @, as in kejohnson@mayerbrown.com.

.edu   Top-level domain that, as part of a domain name (e.g., uiuc.edu), indicates that the host computer is run by an educational institution.

emoticons   Special text inserted in messages, such as <grin> and <sigh>, to show the emotion of the author.

F2F   E-mail abbreviation for "face to face."

FAQ   Abbreviation for "Frequently Asked Questions." Typically a list of common questions and answers for new Internet users or new subscribers to mailing lists.

filter   A set of rules on how to handle incoming e-mail messages that runs automatically. Filters have many uses, like moving messages to a different folder, automatically sending a reply, and the like.

flame   A malicious and often personal attack on the author of an e-mail message. One flame message can lead to a "flame war," which means a series of flames.

FYI   E-mail abbreviation for "for your information."

gateway   A computer system that transfers data (e.g., e-mail) between two normally incompatible networks, converting the data so that each network understands it. For example, a gateway might connect the Internet with an internal e-mail system within a law firm.

.gov   Top-level domain that, as part of a domain name, indicates that the host computer is run by a United States government body.

host   A computer that allows users to communicate with other computers on a network such as the Internet. An Internet host has a unique domain name and IP address.

HTML   HyperText Markup Language. The language used to create World Wide Web documents. HTML support in mail programs allows for formatted messages, using attributes such as font sizes, boldface, and justification.

hypertext   A link between one Internet resource and another, where selecting the link moves the user from the first resource (e.g., a Web page) to the second resource (e.g., a file transfer). For example, a link to a Web page could be embedded in an e-mail message, and clicking on the link would load that page into your Web browser. Likewise, a "mailto" link in a Web page would open up an e-mail message.

IMAP4   Internet Message Access Protocol. A next-generation Internet protocol for retrieving mail from a server. It is often seen as a replacement for the POP3 mail protocol. With IMAP4, mail is stored on the server rather than being downloaded to your computer, thereby making remote access easier.

IMHO   E-mail abbreviation for "in my humble opinion," which rarely means humble.

IP   Internet Protocol. A protocol allowing data to move though multiple networks.

ISP   Internet service provider. The company or organization that provides connections to the Internet.

key   A string of bits used to encrypt and decrypt messages. PGP uses two keys, a public key to encrypt and a private key to decrypt.

Listproc   A program that manages and runs mailing lists.

LISTSERV   A commercial program that manages and runs mailing lists.

LOL   E-mail abbreviation for "laughing out loud." For a more emotional response, see **ROTFL**.

lurk   Regularly reading messages from a mailing list without ever contributing to it. Because mailing list members rarely know all the subscribers, lurkers are virtually invisible. Lurkers are often looked down upon because they take from the list discussions but never contribute to them. However, lurking is an acceptable thing to do when first subscribing to a list, while getting a feel for how the list works and the discussions that take place.

mailing list   A special kind of e-mail function, whereby messages to an address are redistributed to a list of subscribers.

Majordomo   A free UNIX program that manages and runs mailing lists.

.mil   Top-level domain that, as part of a domain name, indicates that the host computer is run by the United States military.

MIME   Multipurpose Internet Mail Extensions. An e-mail protocol that supports sending formatted text and attachments—anything beyond straight ASCII text.

Netiquette   Standards and procedures for "proper" behavior in cyberspace. It can be more specifically divided into e-mail Netiquette, mailing list Netiquette, newsgroup Netiquette, and the like. Most Netiquette is common sense (e.g., be nice), but some is specific, like not posting blatant advertising to a mailing list.

.org   Top-level domain name that is designated for entities that do not fit under any of the other top-level domains, such as com, edu, and gov. Often used for noncommercial organizations.

PGP   Pretty Good Privacy, an encryption technology developed by Philip Zimmermann. PGP uses public and private keys to allow encrypted messages to be exchanged between two people so that only they can decode and read.

plug-in   An add-on program that provides additional functionality to an application program such as e-mail. For example, PGP for Personal Privacy for Eudora is a plug-in that will encrypt messages that you send and decrypt encoded messages that you receive.

POP or POP3   Post Office Protocol. A protocol allowing your mail program to contact the mail server and receive messages using a POP-compatible e-mail program. Sending mail is handled by SMTP.

posting   The act of sending an e-mail message, used typically when sending to a mailing list (e.g., "In Ross's post of last week, he said Word-Perfect was greater than sliced bread. . . .").

PPP   Point-to-Point Protocol. PPP allows a computer to use TCP/IP to connect to and become a node on the Internet through a modem and phone line. PPP replaces the older protocol of SLIP.

private key   The complementary key to a public key in PGP. When someone sends a PGP-encrypted message to you, that party uses your public key to encrypt the message; you use your private key to decrypt it. As the name indicates, you keep your private key private. The private key is protected with its own password, called a passphrase, to prevent unauthorized people from using it.

protocol   A definition of the way in which computers talk to one another and the format of the data they transmit. Standard protocols allow different computers and computers with different operating systems and software to communicate.

public key   The complementary key to your private key in PGP. When someone sends a PGP-encrypted message to you, that party uses your public key to encrypt the message; likewise, when you send a message, you use the recipient's public key for encryption. As the name indicates, you make your public key known to the world.

ROTFL   E-mail abbreviation for "rolling on the floor, laughing."

RTFM   E-mail abbreviation (that is often insulting) for "Read the Fine Manual," although often a different "F" adjective is intended. Typically, the response when someone asks a question that is easily answered in the software's manual or help file.

signature   Lines of text (sometimes in a separate file) that are automatically inserted at the end of an e-mail message when sending it. Signatures typically include the sender's name and e-mail address. They often include affiliation, phone and fax numbers, street address, and silly or profound quotes.

SLIP   Serial Line Internet Protocol. A protocol allowing a computer to connect to the Internet through a modem and phone line. SLIP is being superseded by PPP.

smileys   Smiling faces made by keyboard characters to show humor, irony, or surprise. For example (turn your head sideways),
:-) is smiling
;-) is a wink
:-(is a frown.

S/MIME   Secure MIME (Multipurpose Internet Mail Extensions). An extension to MIME that supports sending encrypted messages, as well as digital signatures, over the Internet. This encryption uses digital certificates, your own and one for each person with whom you are exchanging encrypted mail.

SMTP   Simple Mail Transfer Protocol. The method by which Internet mail is transmitted from one computer to another.

snail mail   Non-electronic mail, typically that stuff delivered by the U.S. Postal Service.

snail mail address   Used for non-electronic mail delivery. Mine is Mayer, Brown & Platt, 190 South LaSalle Street, Chicago, IL 60603.

spam   Junk e-mail. Such unsolicited mail is sent to many users at one time and typically consists of advertisements, "get rich quick" schemes, and invitations for adult services on the Internet. The name comes from the Monty Python skit in which everyone kept singing, "Spam, spam,

spam, spam, spam, spam, spam, spam." Filters can sometimes get rid of certain spam messages before you see them.

T1   A high-speed telephone trunk line that can transmit data at 1.544 megabits per second (Mbps). ISPs should have a T1 or T3 connection to the Internet.

T3   A very high-speed telephone trunk line that can transmit data at 44.7 megabits per second (Mbps).

TCP/IP   Transmission Control Protocol/Internet Protocol. A group of protocols that provide a common way of communicating and sharing data across the Internet.

thread   A series of responses to the original message. By reading through the replies, you can see how the discussion has evolved.

TIA   E-mail abbreviation for "thanks in advance."

TLA   Three-letter acronym, such as BTW and PPP (and, come to think of it, TLA).

TTFN   E-mail abbreviation for "ta ta for now."

URL   Uniform Resource Locator. A unique address identifying an Internet resource, such as a Web page.

UUEncode/UUDecode   An older attachment encoding/decoding program, which is supported by most e-mail systems. Binary files are converted into ASCII text and put into the mail message when sending it; on the receiver's end, UUDecode converts the text back to the binary file.

Winsock   Short for Windows Socket, a program that allows Microsoft Windows programs to work with TCP/IP directly to connect to the Internet.

APPENDIX **D**

Additional
Online Resources

The Internet and e-mail programs are developing so rapidly that printed material can quickly become outdated. Your best reference source is often the Web, since the documents there can be updated more easily. This appendix lists online reference materials that are particularly relevant to the topics discussed in this book.

General E-mail Reference
http://www.yahoo.com/Computers_and_Internet/
Communications_and_Networking/Electronic_Mail
> Yahoo's directory of e-mail resources on the Web.

http://www.webfoot.com/advice/email.top.html
> A Beginner's Guide to Effective E-mail.

Domain Names and Internet Service Providers
http://rs.internic.net/rs-internic.html
> InterNIC Domain Name Registration Services.

http://rs.internic.net/domain-info/nic-rev03.html
> A statement of InterNIC's Domain Name Dispute Policy.

http://rs.internic.net/glossary/index.html
> InterNIC's glossary of domain registration-related terms and organizations.

http://thelist.iworld.com
> "The List" of ISPs, by name, area code, and geographic area.

Eudora

http://www.eudora.com
> Qualcomm's Eudora home page.

http://www.eudora.com/eudoralight/download.html
> Download Eudora Light.

http://www.eudora.com/pro_email/toolkit/pgp.html
> PGP plug-in for Eudora.

Microsoft Internet Explorer

http://www.microsoft.com/ie/download
> Download Microsoft Internet Explorer, including Outlook Express
> (IE 4.0) and Internet Mail and News (IE 3.0).

http://www.microsoft.com/ie/ie40/oe
> The Outlook Express home page.

http://www.microsoft.com/ie/ie40/download/addon.htm
> Download Outlook Express, without the Internet Explorer browser.

http://www.microsoft.com/ie/most/howto/mailnews.htm
> Product information for Microsoft Internet Mail and News for
> Windows 95 and Windows NT 4.0.

http://www.microsoft.com/ie/win31/features/imn.htm
> Product information for Microsoft Internet Mail and News for
> Windows 3.1 and Windows NT 3.51.

Netscape Navigator

http://home.netscape.com/try/download/index.html
> Download Netscape Communicator and Netscape Navigator,
> including Internet E-mail.

http://search.netscape.com/eng/mozilla/Gold/handbook/docs/mnb.html
> The Netscape Navigator Gold (Navigator 3.0) Handbook on Mail.

http://help.netscape.com/kb/client/970615-7.html
> How to create a mailing list in Netscape Messenger.

http://help.netscape.com/kb/client/970615-5.html
> How to create mail filters in Netscape Messenger.

http://help.netscape.com/kb/client/970709-1.html
> How to convert Internet Explorer Mail to Netscape Messenger.

http://help.netscape.com/kb/client/961024-8.html
> How to convert Eudora messages for use in Netscape Messenger.

Web-based E-mail

http://mail.yahoo.com
> Free e-mail, accessible through any Web browser.

http://www.emumail.net
> EmuMail, which allows you to read e-mail from your POP account, using a Web browser.

http://www.mailstart.com
> MailStart.Com, another service for checking your e-mail from any Web browser.

E-mail Address Directories

http://yahoo.four11.com
> The Yahoo White Pages.

http://www.bigfoot.com
> E-mail addresses (and white page listings), searchable by name and region.

http://www.iaf.net
> Internet @ddress.finder, searchable by name and e-mail address.

Netiquette

http://www.dtcc.edu/cs/rfc1855.html
> RFC 1855 (Request for Comments) on Netiquette Guidelines, from Sally Hambridge of Intel Corporation.

http://www.wp.com/fredfish/Netiq.html
> Business Netiquette, focusing on company-to-company e-mail exchange.

http://www.claris.com/products/claris/emailer/eguide/index.html
> Claris Corporation's Guide to E-mail Etiquette.

Mailing Lists

http://www.lib.uchicago.edu/~llou/lawlists/info.html
> Information page for Lyonette Louis-Jacques's comprehensive legal mailing list database, the Law Lists.

http://www.lib.uchicago.edu/~llou/lawlists/intro.html
> Introduction to Lyonette Louis-Jacques's Law Lists.

http://www.lib.uchicago.edu/cgi-bin/law-lists
> Keyword search page for Lyonette Louis-Jacques's Law Lists.

http://www.regent.edu/lawlib/lists/list-law.html
> Regent University Law School's law-related LISTSERVS, including LISTSERV basics, LISTSERV Netiquette, and LISTSERV listings alphabetically and by topic.

http://www.abanet.org/discussions
> Catalog of discussion groups running on the American Bar Association's abanet.org Web server.

http://www.legalminds.org/
> LegalMinds, an archive of many public-interest mailing lists, provided by the FindLaw search site.

http://www.lawguru.com/subscribe/listtool.html
> LawGuru.Com's Mailing List Manager, which provides a forms-based method of subscribing, unsubscribing, and sending commands to more than 500 mailing lists.

http://lawwww.cwru.edu/cwrulaw/faculty/milles/mailser.html
> Information from James Milles, Case Western Reserve University Law Library, on mailing lists and the common mailing list manager commands.

http://www.liszt.com
> Searchable directory of more than 70,000 listserv, listproc, majordomo, and independently managed mailing lists.

E-mail Attachments

http://www.wwwscribe.com/eattach.htm
> "E-mail and Attachments," an article by the author on attachments (originally published in the *Internet Lawyer*).

http://www.pcworld.com/software_lib/data/articles/internet/1770.html
> Download Win Code 2.7.

http://www6.zdnet.com/cgi-bin/texis/swlib/hotfiles/info.html?fcode=00064M
> Download ESS-Code, from Electric Storm Software (Windows 3.1 version).

http://www6.zdnet.com/cgi-bin/texis/swlib/hotfiles/info.html?fcode=0001LZ
> Download ESS-Code, from Electric Storm Software (Windows 95 version).

http://www.powerconcorp.com/info/utils/icode300.zip
> Download InterCode for Windows (ICODE).

PGP
http://www.eudora.com/pro_email/toolkit/pgp.html
> PGP for Personal Privacy plug-in for Eudora Pro.

http://www.nai.com/default_pgp.asp
> The PGP Home page.

http://www.CompLaw.com/pgp.html
> The PGP Awareness Project, to help lawyers learn more about PGP. Run by Samuel Lewis of Romanik, Lavin, Huss & Paoli and member of the Florida Bar's Computer Law Committee.

E-mail Ethics Issues
http://www.legalethics.com
> Peter Krakaur's LegalEthics.Com, which provides a wealth of information on ethics opinions regarding e-mail.

http://www.legalethics.com/states.htm
> Summaries of states' ethics opinions, many relating to e-mail.

http://www.llrx.com/features/e-mail.htm
> Peter Krakaur's argument against mandatory encryption of attorney-client communications.

http://www.interlegal.com
> Interlegal.Com, maintained by lawyer Susan B. Ross, a frequent speaker and writer on ethical issues of using the Internet. Includes articles on e-mail, encryption, and discovery procedures.

http://www.collegehill.com/ilp-news/ross-email.html
> "E-mail: How Attorneys Are Changing the Way They Communicate," by Susan Ross. Discusses practical and ethical issues associated with e-mail use by lawyers.

http://www.legalethics.com/articles/lapidus1.htm
> "Professional Responsibility and Confidentiality Considerations When Using the Internet," by Mary Frances Lapidus.

http://www.legalethics.com/articles/freivogel.htm
> "Internet Communications, Part II, A Larger Perspective" (originally published in *ALAS Loss Prevention Journal*), by William Freivogel. Discusses the issue of encrypting Internet communications.

http://www.computerbar.org/netethics/bjones.htm
> "Client Confidentiality: A Lawyer's Duties with Regard to Internet E-mail," by Robert L. Jones.

http://www.abelaw.com/bamsl/lpm/email.htm
"E-mail and the Attorney-Client Privilege," by Arthur Smith.

http://www.collegehill.com/ilp-news/krakaur3.html
"Ethical Considerations for Internet Use Policies," by Peter Krakaur.

http://www.nlrg.com/lawlet/iup.htm
Internet Acceptable Use Policy, from the National Legal Research Group.

E-Mail Virus Hoaxes
http://ciac.llnl.gov/ciac/CIACHoaxes.html
A summary of e-mail virus hoaxes from the Department of Energy's Computer Incident Advisory Capability (CIAC).

Junk E-mail
http://www.interaccess.com/newsletter/july97/bitstreamcontents/article2.shtml
and
http://www.interaccess.com/newsletter/august97/bitstreamcontents/article1.shtml
One ISP's comments on spam.

http://www.cauce.org
The Coalition Against Unsolicited Commercial E-mail home page.

http://www.zdnet.com/anchordesk/story/story_1693.html
New ways to stop spam, from Jesse Berst of ZDNet.

http://com.primenet.com/spamking
The Netizen's Guide to Spam, Abuse, and Internet Advertising.

http://spam.abuse.net
A "Fight Spam on the Internet" informational page, including frequently asked questions and practical tools for fighting spam. Called the granddaddy of anti-spam sites.

http://spam.abuse.net/howtocomplain.html
Information on how to complain to the spammer's ISP.

Index

Selected Books From . . .
THE LAW PRACTICE MANAGEMENT SECTION

ABA Guide to Lawyer Trust Accounts. This book deals with how lawyers should manage trust accounts to comply with ethical & statutory requirements.

ABA Guide to Professional Managers in the Law Office. This book shows how professional management can and does work. It shows lawyers how to practice more efficiently by delegating management tasks to professional managers.

Billing Innovations. This book examines how innovative fee arrangements and your approach toward billing can deeply affect the attorney-client relationship. It also explains how billing and pricing are absolutely intertwined with strategic planning, maintaining quality of services, marketing, instituting a compensation system, and firm governance.

Changing Jobs, 2nd Ed. A handbook designed to help lawyers make changes in their professional careers. Includes career planning advice from nearly 50 experts.

Compensation Plans for Law Firms, 2nd Ed. This second edition discusses the basics for a fair and simple compensation system for partners, of counsel, associates, paralegals, and staff.

Computer-Assisted Legal Research: A Guide to Successful Online Searching. Covers the fundamentals of LEXIS®-NEXIS® and WESTLAW®, including practical information such as: logging on and off; formulating your search; reviewing results; modifying a query; using special features; downloading documents.

Connecting with Your Client. Written by a psychologist, therapist, and legal consultant, this book presents communications techniques that will help ensure client cooperation and satisfaction.

Do-It-Yourself Public Relations. A hands-on guide for lawyers with public relations ideas, sample letters and forms. The book includes a diskette that includes model letters to the press that have paid off in news stories and media attention.

Finding the Right Lawyer. This guide answers the questions people should ask when searching for legal counsel. It includes a glossary of legal specialties and the ten questions you should ask a lawyer before hiring.

Flying Solo: A Survival Guide for the Solo Lawyer, 2nd ed. An updated and expanded guide to the problems and issues unique to the solo practitioner.

How to Draft Bills Clients Rush to Pay. A collection of techniques for drafting bills that project honesty, competence, fairness and value.

How to Start and Build a Law Practice, 3rd ed. Jay Foonberg's classic guide has been updated and expanded. Included are more than 10 new chapters on marketing, financing, automation, practicing from home, ethics and professional responsibility.

Visit our Web site:
http//www.abanet.org/lpm/catalog

To order: Call Toll-Free 1-800-285-2221

Law Office Policy and Procedures Manual, 3rd Ed. Provides a model for law office policies and procedures. It covers law office organization, management, personnel policies, financial management, technology, and communications systems. Includes diskette.

The Lawyer's Guide to Creating Web Pages. A practical guide that clearly explains HTML, covers how to design a Web site, and introduces Web-authoring tools.

The Lawyer's Guide to the Internet. A guide to what the Internet is (and isn't), how it applies to the legal profession, and the different ways it can -- and should -- be used.

The Lawyer's Guide to Marketing on the Internet. This book talks about the pluses and minuses of marketing on the Internet, as well as how to develop an Internet marketing plan.

The Lawyer's Quick Guide to Microsoft® Internet Explorer; The Lawyer's Quick Guide to Netscape® Navigator. These two guides offer special introductory instructions on the most popular Internet browsers. Four quick and easy lessons including: Basic Navigation, Setting a Bookmark, Browsing with a Purpose, Keeping What You Find.

The Lawyer's Quick Guide to WordPerfect® 7.0/8.0 for Windows®. This easy-to-use guide offers lessons on multitasking, entering and editing text, formatting letters, creating briefs, and more. Perfect for training, this book includes a diskette with practice exercises and word templates.

Leaders' Digest: A Review of the Best Books on Leadership. This book will help you find the best books on leadership to help you achieve extraordinary and exceptional leadership skills.

Living with the Law: Strategies to Avoid Burnout and Create Balance. This multi-author book is intended to help lawyers manage stress, make the practice of law more satisfying, and improve client service.

Practicing Law Without Clients: Making a Living as a Freelance Lawyer. This book describes the freelance legal researching, writing, and consulting opportunities that are available to lawyers.

Running a Law Practice on a Shoestring. Targeted to the solo or small firm lawyer, this book offers a crash course in successful entrepreneurship. Features money-saving tips on office space, computer equipment, travel, furniture, staffing, and more.

Survival Guide for Road Warriors. A guide to using a notebook computer and combinations of equipment and technology so lawyers can be effective in their office, on the road, in the courtroom or at home.

Through the Client's Eyes. Includes an overview of client relations and sample letters, surveys, and self-assessment questions to gauge your client relations acumen.

Women Rainmakers' 101+ Best Marketing Tips. A collection of over 130 marketing tips suggested by women rainmakers throughout the country. Includes tips on image, networking, public relations, and advertising.

Order Form

Qty	Title	LPM Price	Regular Price	Total
_____	ABA Guide to Lawyer Trust Accounts (5110374)	$ 69.95	$ 79.95	$_____
_____	ABA Guide to Prof. Managers in the Law Office (5110373)	69.95	79.95	$_____
_____	Billing Innovations (5110366)	124.95	144.95	$_____
_____	Changing Jobs, 2nd Ed. (5110334)	49.95	59.95	$_____
_____	Compensation Plans for Lawyers, 2nd Ed. (5110353)	69.95	79.95	$_____
_____	Computer-Assisted Legal Research (5110388)	69.95	79.95	$_____
_____	Connecting with Your Client (5110378)	54.95	64.95	$_____
_____	Do-It-Yourself Public Relations (5110352)	69.95	79.95	$_____
_____	Finding the Right Lawyer (5110339)	19.95	19.95	$_____
_____	Flying Solo, 2nd Ed. (5110328)	59.95	69.95	$_____
_____	How to Draft Bills Clients Rush to Pay (5110344)	39.95	49.95	$_____
_____	How to Start & Build a Law Practice, 3rd Ed. (5110293)	32.95	39.95	$_____
_____	Law Office Policy & Procedures Manual (5110375)	99.95	109.95	$_____
_____	Lawyer's Guide to Creating Web Pages (5110383)	54.95	64.95	$_____
_____	Lawyer's Guide to the Internet (5110343)	24.95	29.95	$_____
_____	Lawyer's Guide to Marketing on the Internet (5110371)	54.95	64.95	$_____
_____	Lawyer's Quick Guide to Microsoft Internet® Explorer (5110392)	24.95	29.95	$_____
_____	Lawyer's Quick Guide to Netscape® Navigator (5110384)	24.95	29.95	$_____
_____	Lawyer's Quick Guide to WordPerfect® 7.0/8.0 (5110395)	34.95	39.95	$_____
_____	Leaders' Digest (5110356)	49.95	59.95	$_____
_____	Living with the Law (5110379)	59.95	69.95	$_____
_____	Practicing Law Without Clients (5110376)	49.95	59.95	$_____
_____	Running a Law Practice on a Shoestring (5110387)	39.95	49.95	$_____
_____	Survival Guide for Road Warriors (5110362)	24.95	29.95	$_____
_____	Through the Client's Eyes (5110337)	69.95	79.95	$_____
_____	Women Rainmakers' 101+ Best Marketing Tips (5110336)	14.95	19.95	$_____

*HANDLING	**TAX		
$10.00-$24.99 ... $3.95	DC residents add 5.75%	SUBTOTAL:	$_____
$25.00-$49.99 ... $4.95	IL residents add 8.75%	*HANDLING:	$_____
$50.00+ $5.95	MD residents add 5%	**TAX:	$_____
		TOTAL:	$_____

PAYMENT

☐ Check enclosed (to the ABA)   ☐ Bill Me

☐ Visa ☐ MasterCard ☐ American Express   Account Number:_____

Exp. Date:_____ Signature_____

Name_____

Firm_____

Address_____

City_____ State_____ ZIP_____

Phone number_____

Mail to: ABA Publication Orders   **Phone:** (800) 285-2221   **Fax:** (312) 988-5568
P.O. Box 10892
Chicago, IL 60610-0892   **World Wide Web:** http//www.abanet.org/lpm/catalog
Email: abasvcctr@abanet.org

 THE SECTION OF
LAW PRACTICE
MANAGEMENT

CUSTOMER COMMENT FORM

 ABA

Title of Book: _____

We've tried to make this publication as useful, accurate, and readable as possible. Please take 5 minutes to tell us if we succeeded. Your comments and suggestions will help us improve our publications. Thank you!

1. How did you acquire this publication:

☐ by mail order   ☐ at a meeting/convention   ☐ as a gift

☐ by phone order   ☐ at a bookstore   ☐ don't know

☐ other: (describe) _____
_____

Please rate this publication as follows:

	Excellent	Good	Fair	Poor	Not Applicable
Readability: Was the book easy to read and understand?	☐	☐	☐	☐	☐
Examples/Cases: Were they helpful, practical? Were there enough?	☐	☐	☐	☐	☐
Content: Did the book meet your expectations? Did it cover the subject adequately?	☐	☐	☐	☐	☐
Organization and clarity: Was the sequence of text logical? Was it easy to find what you wanted to know?	☐	☐	☐	☐	☐
Illustrations/forms/checklists: Were they clear and useful? Were there enough?	☐	☐	☐	☐	☐
Physical attractiveness: What did you think of the appearance of the publication (typesetting, printing, etc.)?	☐	☐	☐	☐	☐

Would you recommend this book to another attorney/administrator? ☐ Yes ☐ No

How could this publication be improved? What else would you like to see in it?
_____
_____
_____

Do you have other comments or suggestions? _____
_____
_____

Name _____
Firm/Company _____
Address _____
City/State/Zip _____
Phone _____
Firm Size: _____ Area of specialization: _____

We appreciate your time and help.

Fold

NO POSTAGE
NECESSARY
IF MAILED
IN THE
UNITED STATES

BUSINESS REPLY MAIL

FIRST CLASS   PERMIT NO. 16471   CHICAGO, ILLINOIS

POSTAGE WILL BE PAID BY ADDRESSEE

AMERICAN BAR ASSOCIATION
PPM, 8th FLOOR
750 N. LAKE SHORE DRIVE
CHICAGO, ILLINOIS 60611-9851

Fold

AMERICAN BAR ASSOCIATION

Law Practice Management Section

Membership Application

Access to all these information resources and discounts – for just $3.33 a month!

Membership dues are just $40 a year – just $3.33 a month.
You probably spend more on your general business magazines and newspapers.
But they can't help you succeed in building and managing your practice
like a membership in the ABA Law Practice Management Section.
Make a small investment in success. Join today!

☑ **Yes!** **I want to join the ABA Section of Law Practice Management Section** and gain access to information helping me add more clients, retain and expand business with current clients, and run my law practice more efficiently and competitively!

Check the dues that apply to you:

❑ $40 for ABA members   ❑ $5 for ABA Law Student Division members

Choose your method of payment:

❑ Check enclosed (make payable to American Bar Association)
❑ Bill me
❑ Charge to my: ❑ VISA®   ❑ MASTERCARD®   ❑ AMEX®

Card No.: _____   Exp. Date: _____

Signature: _____   Date: _____

ABA I.D.*: _____
(* Please note: Membership in ABA is a prerequisite to enroll in ABA Sections.)

Name: _____

Firm/Organization: _____

Address: _____

City/State/ZIP: _____

Telephone No.: _____   Fax No.: _____

Primary Email Address: _____

Get Ahead. 🏃

AMERICAN BAR ASSOCIATION ⫯⫯⫯ Law Practice Management Section

Save time by Faxing or Phoning!

▶ Fax your application to: (312) 988-5820
▶ Join by phone if using a credit card: (800) 285-2221 (ABA1)
▶ Email us for more information at: lpm@abanet.org
▶ Check us out on the Internet: http://www.abanet.org/lpm

750 N. LAKE SHORE DRIVE
CHICAGO, IL 60611
PHONE: (312) 988-5619
FAX: (312) 988-5820
Email: lpm@abanet.org

I understand that Section dues include a $24 basic subscription to Law Practice Management; this subscription charge is not deductible from the dues and additional subscriptions are not available at this rate. Membership dues in the American Bar Association are not deductible as charitable contributions for income tax purposes. However, such dues may be deductible as a business expense.